Object-Oriented Programming in Visual Basic

James W. Cooper

Steve Wilent, Editor

Pinnacle Publishing, Inc.

Brent P. Smith	*Publisher*
Steve Wilent	*Series Editor*
Rod Stephens	*Technical Editor*

Published by Pinnacle Publishing Inc.
PO Box 888, Kent, WA 98035-0888
206-251-1900
800-788-1900
206-251-5057 (fax)

In Europe contact:
Tomalin Associates
The Gables
Vine Street
Great Bardfield
Essex CM7 4SR
United Kingdom
371-81-1299
371-81-1283 (fax)

ISBN 1-880935-49-X

Library of Congress Cataloging-in-Publication Data available

Publishing coordination and book production by
Laing Communications Inc., Redmond, Washington, and Edmonton, Alberta

Sandra J. Harner	*Design*
Kelly C. Rush	*Production*
Laura Dickinson	*Editorial Coordination*
Christine Laing	
Billie Jo Bouic	*Copyediting*

To my wife, Vicki, who had the determination to return to academia and get her Master's in social work while I was writing this manuscript.

Contents

Preface

This book is written for programmers who want to learn about object-oriented programming in Microsoft Visual Basic 4. If you have worked in earlier versions of VB, you can skip parts of Chapters 1 and 2. If you haven't, you probably will be able to learn almost all you need to get started from this book. If you are in doubt about how to use any keyword or syntax, you can point to the keyword and press F1 to get to fairly extensive help. In addition, you can consult other books in this series or any introductory book on Visual Basic to get started.

You will find every program in this book on the accompanying example disk. You will probably learn the most if you try to write some of the programs before going to the samples on the disk, but you can use these code examples as prototypes to get you started writing your own programs.

Acknowledgments

I'd like to acknowledge the Wilton Y Wahoo Swim Team for providing a venue where I learned much of this material and for providing data for some of the examples. I'd like to thank the Special Olympics World Games Organizing Committee for the opportunity to work with them and for providing an excuse to learn about databases in Microsoft Visual Basic.

I'd also like to thank my wife, Vicki, and our children, Vaughn and Nicole, for letting me spend my holiday on this screed, and our pets for providing some of the multimedia clips. I'd particularly like to thank Mike Hudson at Hudson Computer Consulting for his meticulous reading of the manuscript, and my colleagues Steve Gates, Dick Lam, and Lei Kuang at IBM Research for their valuable suggestions.

James W. Cooper
Wilton, CT
January, 1996

1 | We've Come a Long Way Since BASICA

If you last looked into BASIC a few years ago, you might wonder why Visual Basic has become one of the most popular Microsoft Windows-based development languages today. The original BASIC, as described at Dartmouth by John Kemeny and Thomas Kurtz and adopted by Microsoft and IBM into a language shipped in the ROM of early personal computers, was rather limited.

Some of the major objections to BASICA and the related GW-BASIC language were:

- Every line in the program required a line number.
- Branching required use of the infamous GOTO statement, and looping could be accomplished only with FOR...NEXT statements.
- You had to call subroutines using the GOSUB statement, which did not provide a method for passing arguments to that subroutine.
- All variables were global.
- There was no simple way to specify a record or structure containing a group of variables of several types: The FIELD statement did not scale to larger programs.
- There was no variable declaration mechanism: All variables were declared automatically when first used.

Thus, a typical BASICA program might look like this:

```
100 PRINT "Enter Temperature:" ;
110 INPUT T
120 PRINT "Celsius or Fahrenheit:" ;
130 INPUT SCALE$
140 IF SCALE$="C" THEN NEWTEMP=T*9/5+32
150 IF SCALE$="F" THEN NEWTEMP=(T-32)*5/9
160 PRINT "Converted Temp=";NEWTEMP
170 GOTO 100
```

Clearly, BASICA is not a suitable language dialect for professional software development. Of course, we have set up a digital straw man here: All of these objections and a number of others have been removed.

Introducing Visual Basic

The Visual Basic language allows you to write elegant, structured programs as well as manipulate visual aspects of the Windows environment in a simple fashion. We'll rewrite that clunky program for Windows shortly, but first, let's look at some of Visual Basic's language features. You'll see quickly that we aren't in Kansas anymore.

Using If-Then-Else

While the GOTO statement remains part of the Visual Basic language to allow emergency exit from nested loops, you can write programs without ever using it again. Instead, you can make decisions with the expanded If-Then-Else statement:

```
'Computation of simple quadratic formula
discrim = b ^ 2 - 4 * a * c   'calculate the discriminant
If discrim > 0 Then
  y1 = (-b + Sqr(discrim)) / (2 * a)  'find the real roots
  y2 = (-b - Sqr(discrim)) / (2 * a)
  errflag = False
Else
  y1 = 0                'set error if roots
  y2 = 0                'are imaginary
  errflag = True
Endif
```

Multiple decisions with Select Case

If you need to test for one of several possibilities, you can use the Select Case statement. The variables you compare may be integers, floating-point numbers, or strings:

```
Select Case Scale$
  Case "C"
  NewTemp = T * 9 / 5 + 32
  Case "F"
  NewTemp = (T - 32) * 5 / 9
  Case "R"
  NewTemp = (T - 400) * 5 / 9
 Case "K"
  NewTemp = (T - 273.16) * 5 / 9
End Select
```

Looping with While-Wend

In BASICA, you might have to read in a file a line at a time using the awkward construction:

```
100 F = 1           'file variable
110 Open "foo.txt" for input as #f
120 LINE INPUT #F, S$       'read in a line from the file
130 '......                 'Do something with data
140 IF NOT EOF(F) GOTO 110  'Go back until end found
150 CLOSE #F
```

In Visual Basic, you would instead write:

```
f = Freefile            'get next free file number
Open "foo.txt" For Input As #f 'Open the file
While Not Eof(f)                'loop until end of file
  Line Input #f, s$     'read in a line from the file
 '.....                 'do something
Wend
Close #f                'close file
```

Looping with Do-Loop statements

You can write the same code using one of four possible Do-Loop statements:

Note that the Do-While statement is functionally equivalent to the While-Wend statement. The While-Wend statement is more entrenched, but the four Do-Loop statements are part of the American National Standards Institute (ANSI) standard for Basic.

Variable Types in Visual Basic

The Visual Basic variable types are the ones you might expect, and are shown in Table 1-1.

Table 1-1.

Variable types in VB

Type	Bytes	Range
Integer	2	-32,768 to 32,767
Long	4	-2,147,483,648 to 2,147,83,647
Single	4	± (1.401 x 10^{-45} to 3.402 x 10^{38})
Double	8	± (4.940 x 10^{-45} to 1.797 x 10^{308})
String	variable	A character array of up to 64K length
Byte	1	A single 8-bit quantity
Boolean	2	A variable that can be True or False
Currency	8	A fixed-point representation of currency values
Date	8	A representation of any date from 1/1/100 to 12/31/9999
Variant	up to 16	A variable that can take on any of the preceding types

Declaring variables

It is usual, in Visual Basic, to declare the variables in a procedure using the Dim statement:

```
Option Explicit    'require variable declarations
Dim j As Integer, Temp as Single, Fred as String
```

If all variables are declared and if the Option Explicit statement is inserted in every file, Visual Basic will check for you to see that no variables are misspelled or undeclared.

Variable-type characters

You can explicitly declare that a variable is of one of the standard types by terminating it with one of the standard type-specifier characters, shown in Table 1-2.

Table 1-2.

Standard type-specifier characters

$	String
&	Long
%	Integer
!	Single
#	Double
@	Currency

The most common mistake

Some other languages assume that all the variables named in a single declaration have the same type:

```
Dim x, y, z As Integer
```

This is *not* true in Visual Basic. In the example above, x and y are of type Variant, while only z is of type Integer. Be careful in writing your Dim statements.

Variable names

Variable names may be of any reasonable length, up to 255 characters, and must begin with a letter. They can't contain periods or other punctuation characters used to declare a type ($, %, &, or #). You can use capitalization and underscore characters to make a variable's meaning clearer: SumOfPairs and Sum_Of_Pairs are easier to read than sumofpairs.

While Visual Basic variable names are case insensitive, the case you declare a variable or function name in is remembered, and all further instances of that variable name are converted to the mixture of upper and lowercase you selected originally.

Constants

You also can declare a constant of any of these types. Visual Basic deduces the type of the constant from the value it is given:

```
Const Max = 1000       'Integer
Const PI = 3.1416      'Single
Const Mon = "September" 'String
```

Conversion Between Types

In general, Visual Basic will convert the variables in a mixed expression to the highest possible type (single, double) before carrying out the computation. Then, of course, if the target variable is of a lower order, the result is converted back down.

Unexpected type coercion

In Visual Basic 4, unexpected type coercion is carried to much greater extremes than in earlier versions. For example, you would not expect the following statement to be legal:

```
Dim x As Single, j As Integer, s$
  s$ = "2"
  j = 5
  x = j + s$ 'legal in VB 4.0
  Debug.Print x 'prints out "7"
```

Because of this type coercion, the plus (+) symbol sometimes can be dangerous when used to concatenate strings:

```
Frname$ = "Fred"
Lname$ = "Fump"
Fullname$ = Frname$ + " " + Lname$
```

Here, it won't matter, but to prevent coercion when the strings contain numbers, you can use the ampersand (&) symbol for combining strings as well as the plus symbol.

```
Fullname$ = Frname$ & " " & Lname$
```

Versions of Visual Basic

Visual Basic 4 comes in 16-bit and 32-bit versions. Both will run under Windows 95, but the 16-bit version also can run under and generate code for Windows 3.1. The principal purpose of the 16-bit version is to work with existing Visual Basic 3.0 code and upgrade it, as well as produce code for Windows 3.1. The 32-bit version has additional controls that can make your application look more professional, such as a TreeList, a ListView and a Rich Text Box. In addition, the common dialog box has the more professional Windows 95 look.

Visual Basic 4 is shipped in three price versions as well: an entry-level personal version, a Professional Edition and an Enterprise version. The Professional Edition includes the 16- and 32-bit versions of VB and access to databases. The Enterprise version adds a source-code control system and access to remote OLE objects.

Example code disk

The companion disk contains every program discussed in this book. All of them have been tested under both the 16-bit and 32-bit versions of VB 4 under Windows 95, except for those in Chapters 6, 7, and 8 that require controls present only in the 32-bit version.

Setting Up Visual Basic

From the Tools menu, select Options and click the Environment tab, shown in Figure 1-1.

Figure 1-1.

Visual Basic Tools/Options Environment tab

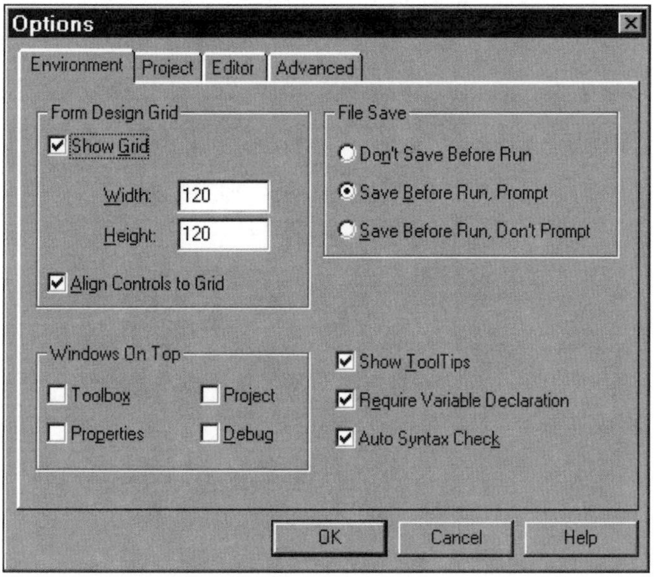

If you select Require Variable Declarations, Visual Basic will insert the Option Explicit declaration in every new module for you. You should also select one of the "Save Before Run" options, so that your changes are always saved to disk before you begin testing a program that might inadvertently cause VB to crash.

It is also important that you do not select Compile on Demand from the Advanced tab, because it leads to situations in which the program starts but exits on the first syntax error, instead of finding all the syntax errors before you begin. This is illustrated in Figure 1-2.

Figure 1-2.

The Tools/Options Advanced tab

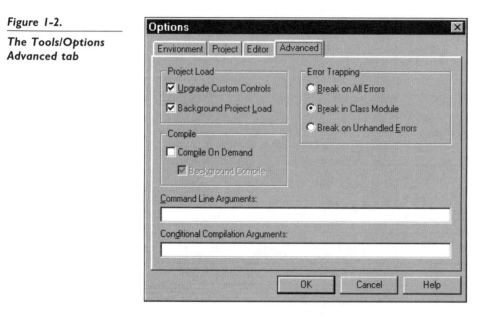

Functions and Subprograms

While BASICA allowed you to call subroutines in the same source code module using only the GOSUB statement, Visual Basic allows you to define and call subprograms and functions in the same or different source code modules and pass arguments to them. Let's make a function out of our quadratic formula program:

```
Function QuadForm (a As Single, b As Single, _
                   c As Single) As Single
Dim discrim As Single

discrim = b ^ 2 - 4 * a * c 'calculate the discriminant
If discrim >= 0 Then        'only take root if positive
  QuadForm = (-b + Sqr(discrim)) / (2 * a)
Else
  QuadForm = 0              'else return zero
End If
End Function
```

You would then call this function by writing:

```
y = QuadForm(a, b, c)
```

Calling by reference and by value

In Visual Basic 4, the default is to pass variables in subprograms by reference, which means that the actual variable can be changed within the subprogram. If you want to ensure that the variables in the calling program will not be changed by the function, you can add the ByVal keyword before each variable that you do not wish to change:

```
Function QuadForm (ByVal a As Single, ByVal b As Single, _
                ByVal c As Single) As Single
```

Note the use of the underscore as a line-continuation character. This is new in Visual Basic 4 but has been used commonly in print for years to allow for narrow column layouts in printed materials.

Optional parameters

Visual Basic 4 also introduces the concept of optional calling parameters. There may be zero or more optional parameters in a subprogram, but they must always be last and must always be of Variant type. Each one must be preceded with the Optional keyword. You can use the function IsMissing to determine whether a parameter exists during that call or not:

```
Public Sub FileWriteln(Optional s As Variant)
'write variable (or not) followed by new line characters
If Not IsMissing(s) Then
  Print #file_handle, s
Else
  Print #file_handle,
End If
End Sub
```

Subprograms

Visual Basic refers to routines starting with the keyword Sub as sub procedures or subprograms, because the now unused GOSUB statement called code that was referred to as subroutines. Most people refer to these sub procedures as subroutines anyway.

A subroutine is just like a function except that it does not return a value to the left of the equals (=) symbol. Let's rewrite this same function to return both roots of a quadratic equation:

```
Sub QuadCalc (y1 As Single, y2 As Single, ByVal a As Single, _
            ByVal b As Single, ByVal c As Single)
Dim discrim As Single
```

Continued on next page

Continued from previous page

```
discrim = b ^ 2 - 4 * a * c 'calculate the discriminant
If discrim >= 0 Then    'only take sqrt if positive
  y1 = (-b + Sqr(discrim)) / (2 * a)
  y2 = (-b - Sqr(discrim)) / (2 * a)
Else
  y1 = 0              'else return zero
  y2 = 0
End If
End Sub
```

Note that y1 and y2 are passed by reference and the input parameters are passed by value.

Alternative syntax for calling subroutines

Visual Basic supports two ways to call subroutines:

```
Call QuadCalc (y1, y2, 3, 4, 5)
```

and

```
QuadCalc y1, y2, 3, 4, 5
```

The first method requires the Call keyword and parentheses around the arguments. The second method often is used in calling internal functions in objects (methods) and omits both the Call and the parentheses. Be careful not to mix the two. If you use parentheses without the Call keyword, Visual Basic attempts to evaluate those parameters as an expression. This can lead to the wrong type or the wrong number of arguments being assumed.

Structured Programming Principles

Now that we have a real language with a formal structure, we can write fairly powerful programs. And we can apply some of the principles of structured programming in our work. Some of these are:

- All variables should be declared by type within the function or subprogram.
- Global variables should be avoided whenever possible.
- Programs should be well commented with comments explaining the program's purpose as well as its individual steps.
- Each subprogram and loop within a program should have only one entry and one exit point.
- Loops should be indented so that their nesting is visually apparent.

- Programs should be designed from the top down, with the most general functions outlined first, and the calls to specific routines written before the routines themselves are written.
- Program routines should not be gullible. They should not assume that input parameters are valid without checking them, or that system functions execute without error.

Avoiding the use of GOTO

The GOTO statement was absolutely necessary in the original specification of BASIC as it was in its precursor, Fortran. However, in a structured language like Visual Basic, you can almost always write code that avoids using it. Remember, any code you write may be read and changed by someone later. Even if the only "someone" is you, it is important that you be able to quickly grasp the purpose of code, and not have to trace through a pasta-like mass of GOTO statements.

One of the most common reasons programmers use GOTO statements is to get out of the middle of deeply nested loops when a pathological error condition occurs. For example, in a matrix inversion routine, you manipulate rows and columns to find the equivalent of a matrix's reciprocal. If, in the process, the matrix determinant becomes zero, the matrix is said to be singular and cannot be inverted. Here is a program fragment from such an inversion:

```
Do
   amax = 0
   For j = 1 To n
    '....
   Next j
    If amax < Tolerance Then 'here we could just exit
      determ = 0    'but instead we set determ=0
    Else
    '...       'do real inversion here
    End If
Loop Until (i > n) Or (determ = 0)   'and make this
                'a loop exit condition
```

In a similar fashion, programmers sometimes use the statements Exit Sub or Exit Function to escape from the middle of a subprogram. Again, setting a flag and exiting at the bottom of the loop makes the code much easier to follow.

In the following chapters, you'll see that Visual Basic provides a number of tools for writing elegant, structured programs. I will begin by discussing the actual visual interface in Chapter 2.

2 | Forms and Programming

Since Visual Basic is, of course, primarily a visual language to write Windows-based programs with, we will now illustrate how to write a simple one-form and a two-form program. We'll see in this chapter how to design the forms and fields that make up most Visual Basic windows, and discuss the concepts of event-driven programming.

Temperature Conversion

Let's start Visual Basic by double-clicking its icon or choosing it from the Windows 95 Start Programs menu. This will bring up a blank form, labeled "Form1." You are now in Visual Basic design mode, when you can insert controls on blank forms to create the dialog boxes that make up most of Visual Basic programming. If you press F4 or select View/Properties, you will bring up that form's Properties window as shown in Figure 2-1. The toolbox of available controls to put on that form is shown on the left of the window.

First, change the form caption to "Temperature Conversion" by typing the new caption in the Caption box of the Properties window. Then type "TempCalc" in the Name box as shown in Figure 2-2.

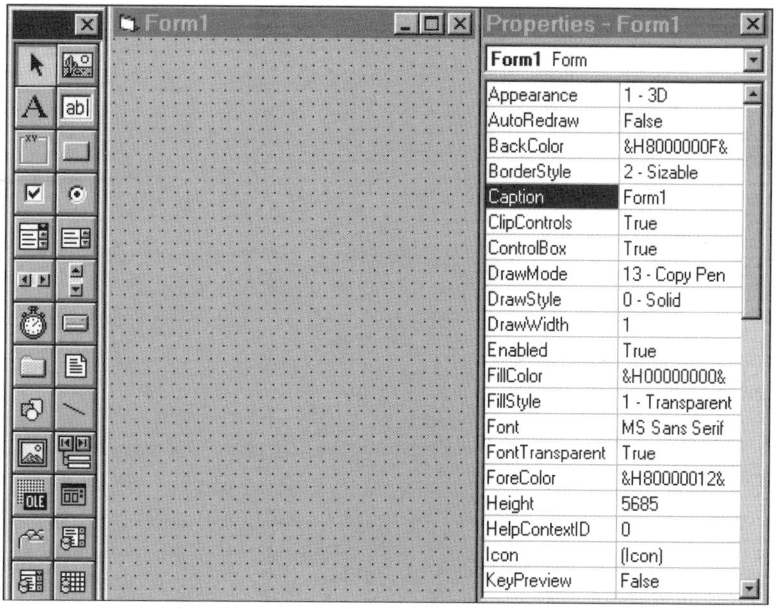

Figure 2-1.

The toolbox, a blank form, and the Properties window

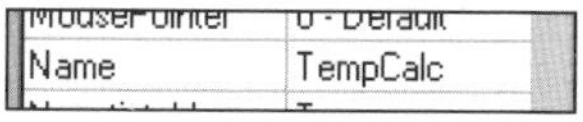

Figure 2-2.

Setting the Name property to "TempCalc"

Now you're ready to put some controls on the form. All the controls you'll need are represented by buttons in the control toolbox. You can find out what they do by pointing to them until the ToolTip box describing their purpose appears.

You are going to build the form shown in Figure 2-3 as a program to convert temperatures between Fahrenheit and Celsius. Follow these steps:

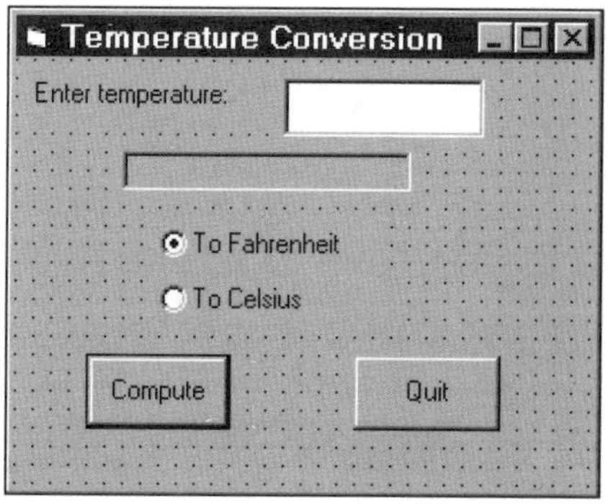

Figure 2-3.

Design of the TempCalc Form

1. Create labels for the form by clicking the button marked "A" in the toolbox.
2. Create one and change its caption to "Enter temperature:".
3. Click the Text Box button and insert an edit field to the right of that label.
4. Change the field Text property to blank and change the field name to "Input_temp."
5. Place a label field with the caption set to blank below that and change its name to "Result."
6. Insert two Option buttons labeled "To Fahrenheit" and "To Celsius" below them, and name them "Fahr" and "Celsius."
7. Change the Value property of the Fahr button to True so that it is already selected.
8. Insert two command buttons labeled "Compute" and "Quit." Put these same words in their Name fields.
9. Finally, change the Default property of the Compute button to True and the Cancel property of the Quit button to True. These properties mean that the Compute button will be activated whenever the user presses ENTER and the Quit button will be activated whenever the user presses ESC.

Writing the code

This looks like a simple form design for a simple project. However, you haven't written any code yet. And, in fact, you have to write precious little code for this program to work. The code you need to write simply describes what happens when the user clicks Compute and Quit. You can write that code now by simply double-clicking those two buttons.

First double-click Quit. This will bring up a code window with the following code already written for you:

```
Private Sub Quit_Click()


End Sub
```

To complete this simple procedure, just insert an End statement:

```
Private Sub Quit_Click()
 End
End Sub
```

Then, to write the code executed when the Compute button is pressed, double-click it and fill in the following code:

```
Private Sub Compute_Click()
Dim newtemp As Single, temp As Single
```

Continued on next page

```
temp = Val(input_temp.Text)
If Fahr.Value Then      'is Fahr button down?
  newtemp = 9 * (temp / 5) + 32
Else            'no, must be Celsius
  newtemp = 5 * (temp - 32) / 9
End If
result.Caption = Str$(newtemp)'display result
End Sub
```

This is the entire program! To execute it, press F5 or click the right triangle (play button) on the toolbar. Type a temperature and click Compute. You will see a complete working program that performs either of the two conversions each time you click Compute. Finally, close the program by clicking Quit. The program TEMPCALC on the companion disk illustrates these features.

Event-Driven Programming

You can now appreciate the term "event-driven" programming. Much of the code written in Visual Basic responds to events like mouse clicks or keystrokes. In the simple program you just wrote, you created two command buttons: Compute and Quit. When a user clicks these buttons, VB generates a Compute_Click or a Quit_Click event. These events then become the subroutines that you write code for in most Visual Basic programs. Common events you can write code for include:

- Click
- MouseDown
- MouseUp
- MouseMove
- GotFocus
- LostFocus
- KeyPress
- KeyDown
- KeyUp
- DragOver
- DragDrop

In most VB programs, you design a few simple forms, allow the user to fill them out and, when the user clicks a command button, execute a Click event subroutine that checks the values of the various form elements and performs whatever operations the program is designed to do.

In summary, in event-driven programming, you present a display form and respond to the events for each of the controls on the form.

Communication Between Forms

Now let's consider a slightly more complicated program that uses two forms, one allowing you to enter the temperatures, and another to plot an array of them in a picture box. You will modify the original program slightly to contain a Show button to display a plot of the temperatures entered so far, as illustrated in Figure 2-4.

Figure 2-4.

TempCalc program shown running

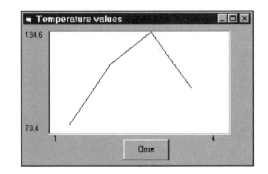

Then, you will make a second form that displays the minimum and maximum values as axis labels and plots the values. To add a form to your project, select Insert/Form from the VB menu, and then bring up its project window by pressing F4 to change its name from Form1 to something more memorable. The new form you will create is shown in Figure 2-5.

Figure 2-5.

Plot of entered temperatures on second form

You now need to design a method for the plotting form to obtain the list of values that were entered in the entry form. You will first do this the way it was done in previous versions of Visual Basic, to illustrate the weakness of this initial approach. In later chapters I will show how object-oriented programming can make this a much simpler and more error-free process. The program discussed throughout this section is the TEMPENTR program on the companion disk.

In Visual Basic, the procedures and data within a form are not visible to the rest of the program, so the plotting form could not simply ask the entry form for its data. Instead, the usual way has been to create a separate Basic code module that contains global data as well as procedures that might be called by many modules. For this program, you create a small module called tempval.bas, which contains the following few lines:

```
Option Explicit


Global temps(10) As Single
Global temp_num As Integer
```

You will set the values into the temp array in the TempEntr module's Computer_Click subroutine as shown below. Then you can access this same array to plot these data from the plotting form.

The data in this module can then be accessed by both the entry form and the plotting form. You modify the entry form click event for the button now labeled Enter to contain the following additional code:

```
Private Sub Compute_Click()
Dim newtemp As Single, temp As Single
temp = Val(input_temp.Text)   'get text from input
If Fahr.Value Then            'see if Fahr is clicked
  newtemp = 9 * (temp / 5) + 32
Else                          'if not it is Celsius
  newtemp = 5 * (temp - 32) / 9
End If
result.Caption = Str$(newtemp)  'put result in
            'Result label
temp_num = temp_num + 1     'count entries
temps(temp_num) = newtemp   'and store in array
input_temp.Text = ""        'clear for next entry
End Sub
```

Then the only other change you need to make in the entry form is a statement in the Click routine for the Show button:

```
Private Sub showit_Click()
  Plottemp.Show              'display plot form
End Sub
```

This loads and displays the plotting form.

The Form_Load event

As noted previously, all Windows programming is event-driven programming under the covers—you write programs to respond to events such as mouse clicks or drags, and the display and dismissal of various windows or forms.

Whenever you begin to display a new form such as the PlotTemp form described below, a Form_Load event occurs. You can insert code in that event to initialize any visual or numerical parameters before the form actually is displayed. In the form loading routine, for example, you initialize the scale for the plot you'll make.

Graphics functions, such as Line or Circle commands, can't take place in a Form_Load event because the display surface they would draw on is not yet active.

The plotting form

The plotting form finds the maximum and minimum value in the temps array and sets the y-scale of the picture box 10 percent larger than that. It sets the x-axis to the number of points in the array and leaves 5 percent room on either side. It also sets the text of the minimum and maximum axis labels.

You can open a code window in which to write code for the Form_Load event by double-clicking anywhere on the background of the form:

```
Private Sub Form_Load()
Dim i As Integer, max As Single, min As Single
Dim x As Single, y As Single
Dim dx As Single, dy As Single


min = 1E+36
max = -1E+36
'find min and max to scale window
For i = 1 To temp_num
  If temps(i) < min Then min = temps(i)
  If temps(i) > max Then max = temps(i)
Next i


'set coordinates 10% larger, making bottom 0,0
Picture1.ScaleHeight = -(max - min) * 1.1
Picture1.ScaleTop = max
Picture1.ScaleWidth = 1.1 * temp_num
Picture1.ScaleLeft = 0.5
```

Continued on next page

```
'set captions for axes
minx.Caption = "1"      'set the x captions
maxx.Caption = Format$(temp_num)
miny.Caption = Format$(min) 'and the y captions
maxy.Caption = Format$(max)
End Sub
```

The actual plotting is carried out after the form is loaded, using the Paint event as a signal to start drawing:

```
Private Sub Form_Paint()
Dim i As Integer
'Drawing this during form load is too soon


Picture1.PSet (1, temps(1))     'set first point
For i = 2 To temp_num
  Picture1.Line -(i, temps(i)) 'plot the rest
Next i
End Sub
```

So, in this simple example you have stored the array of temperatures and the size of that array in global variables that are accessible from any module in the program. When the program is very simple like this one, there is no difficulty in doing this, but when the program contains 25 or more forms and modules, it invites error, since any one of those modules might change those values in the array. More serious is what happens as a program evolves over time and changes need to be made. You find it much more difficult to keep track of which parts of the program are "allowed" to manipulate these global variables. Further, the number of global variables proliferates over time, making program maintenance that much more difficult.

It is these sorts of problems that Visual Basic 4 addresses. We will begin our discussion of object-oriented programming in Chapter 3 and will revisit the temperature program later.

Other Visual Basic Controls

Programming in Visual Basic is, to a large degree, deciding how to represent your information visually and selecting various standard controls for forms, to show the interaction with that information. You already have seen the text box, the label field, the command button and the picture box.

Some other common controls you might use are summarized in Table 2-1.

Table 2-1.

Common VB controls

Control	Purpose
ListBox	Shows a list of text values, one per line
ComboBox	A drop-down list box where the user also can enter text
CheckBox	A box whose value can be on, off, or disabled. You can select one or many check boxes in a group.
Option button	A button that allows you to select only one from a group of choices
Frame	A box that surrounds controls to give them a logical grouping. It also allows you to have several unrelated groups of option buttons.
Shape and Line controls	Tools for drawing lines, squares, rectangles, and circles when designing a form
Drive, Directory, and File boxes	Allows the user to select a drive, directory, and file
Image	A type of picture box that allows display of bitmaps but has fewer features and uses fewer Windows resources than the picture box. It does allow stretching of images to fit the box.
Timer	An invisible control used to cause events to occur at timed intervals
Scroll bars	Horizontal and vertical bars with a scroll box and scroll arrows at either end to move through any sort of data

Examples of the Basic Controls

The program CONTROLS.VBP on the companion disk contains the controls shown in Table 2-1, along with some simple example code for using them. Figure 2-6 shows the CONTROLS.VBP program running.

Figure 2-6.

The CONTROLS.VBP program running

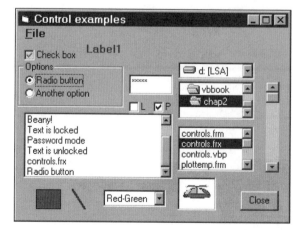

General control properties

Nearly all controls have the common properties shown in Table 2-2.

Table 2-2.

Common control properties

Caption	The text displayed in label and command button controls
Visible	True if shown, False if hidden
Enabled	Setting this property to False makes control inoperative
Font	Clicking the "..." in the Properties window brings up a Font dialog box where you can set the font name, bold, italic, and so forth. You also can set Font.Name, Font.Size, Font.Bold, and Font.Italic from the program itself.
Top, Left	Coordinates at top and left edges on form
Height, Width	Size on form
Forecolor, Backcolor	Color of text and background
Index	If you're using a control array, the Index property indicates which one
MousePointer	Type (1 to 13) of mouse pointer when pointer is over control
Name	Name of control
TabIndex	Relative position when tabbing between controls
TabStop	True if tabbing will stop at this control
Tag	A string for storing your private data
Text	The text data in text boxes, list boxes, and combo boxes

Label

The label is a display of static text. You can change the text as well as the font and color from within the program, but the user can't interact with a label. The Caption property can be changed at run time to display new text:

```
Label1.Caption = "Beany!"
```

While you usually change the Name property of a control to reflect its function, labels are usually the exception, because they are most often set up at design time as labels for parts of a form and never changed again.

TextBox

You already have seen how a text box is used to enter and retrieve data using the Text property. You also can select any part of the text using the SelStart and SelLength properties. If you select all or part of the text and then type in a character, it replaces all the selected text.

In VB 4, the Locked property can be set to True to prevent users from entering new text.

The PasswordChar property replaces the display of any characters typed with the password character. However, the Text property still contains what was actually typed. If the PasswordChar property is set to " ", the text box operates normally.

In the CONTROLS.VBP program on the companion disk, when you tab to the list box the text is highlighted using the SelStart and Sellength properties. You do this by intercepting the GotFocus event as follows:

```
Private Sub Text1_GotFocus()
Text1.SelStart = 0
Text1.SelLength = Len(Text1.Text)
End Sub
```

The L and P check boxes allow you to set the Locked and PasswordChar properties.

Command button

The command button allows you to click a single button to execute a function immediately. The text on a command button is set in the Caption property. One command button per form may have its Default property set, indicating that it will be activated if you press ENTER. One command button per from may have its Cancel property set, indicating that it will be executed if you press ESC. It is common to set some command button's Enabled property to False and set it to True only when the form has been filled in such that that function can reasonably be executed.

In the CONTROLS.VBP program, the Close command button brings up a message box asking if you really want to exit.

ListBox

A list box is a single column of lines of text. If there are more lines than can be displayed, a scroll bar appears along the right side. Be sure to leave room for it in your form design, since it takes up 100 pixels or so.

The major methods for the list box are shown in Table 2-3.

Table 2-3.

Major list box methods

Lb.AddItem *"any string"*	Add line to end of list.
Lb.RemoveItem *i*	Remove item i.
Lb.Clear	Clear list

The major properties include those shown in Table 2-4.

Table 2-4.

Major list box properties

Lb.ListCount	Number of lines in list box
Lb.ListIndex	Index of selected line. Set to -1 if none selected.
Lb.List(i)	The text if the *i*th line (0-count-1)
Lb.Text	The text of the selected line
Lb.MultiSelect	0=single selection, 1=multiple selection, 2=select block with Shift andDownarrow
Lb.Selected (i)	True if line *I* is selected

If MultiSelect is 0, then the selected line is given by the ListIndex property. If it is -1, no line is selected. If a line is selected, then the Text property contains the text of that line, as does Lb.List(Lb.ListIndex). You can add new text to any line by setting LB.List(i) to that text.

If you set the MultiSelect property to 1 or 2, you can find out which are selected only by scanning from 0 to ListCount-1, and testing whether the Selected (i) property is True.

In the CONTROLS.VBP program on the companion disk, you add a line to the list box when you act on nearly every control. If you click a line in the list box, that line is displayed as the label caption.

ComboBox

The combo box has three different styles: the drop-down combo, the drop-down list, and the simple combo. The drop-down combo allows you to type into the text box at the top of the list or to select from a drop-down list. The drop-down list allows you to select only from the drop-down list, and the simple combo allows you display a single line and select from the list by pressing the DOWN ARROW key.

In the CONTROLS.VBP program on the companion disk, the combo box is set to a drop-down list, and you can select between red-green color flashing and blue-yellow color flashing.

CheckBox

The state of the check box is determined by its Value property—its values are shown in Table 2-5.

0	unchecked
1	checked
-1	grayed

VB represents these values by the named constants vbChecked, vbUnchecked, and vbGrayed. Check boxes operate independently of each other and can be used when you want to select one or more from a set of choices. Be careful not to use the construction:

```
If Check1.Value Then
```

to test for whether a check box is selected, since True is represented as -1 in Visual Basic. Instead, always write:

```
If (Check1.value = 1) Then
```

In the CONTROLS.VBP program on the companion disk, the check box starts out grayed by being set in the Form_Load procedure, but can be selected or cleared while running.

Option buttons

Option buttons are used when you want to allow only one of a set of choices. Turning one on always turns any others in the group off.

If you want to have more than one group of option buttons on a form, you should enclose them in a frame as shown in the CONTROLS.VBP program on the companion disk.

The Value parameter of option buttons can take on only the two values True and False, so you can make the logical test:

```
If Option1.Value Then
```

You cannot make the same test using the check box.

Frames

A frame is used to group controls for readability. It also provides a way to have more than one set of option buttons on a single form. To ensure that a control is "inside" a frame and not just on top of it, move the frame in design mode and make sure the controls follow it. If they do not, select all the controls while pressing SHIFT, use the Cut command to delete them, and then select the frame and paste them back in using the Paste command.

You can avoid this problem by ensuring the frame is selected before placing a control inside.

Shapes and lines

You can decorate a form with lines of any thickness and color, or shapes that can be rectangles, squares, ovals, circles, rounded rectangles, or rounded squares. These shapes can be filled with colors or patterns. They are primarily to assist you in designing professional-looking forms—they do not receive any events. In the CONTROLS.VBP program on the companion disk, you change the rectangle's fill color every half second.

Drive, Directory, and File controls

These controls provide a way for you to select a drive, directory, or file name. They are less frequently used than you might at first think, because the Common Dialog control described later in this chapter provides access to the standard Windows File/Open and File/Save menu choices. The Drive control has the single property Drive, which can be set to any letter. If that drive does not exist or does not contain a disk, an error occurs. The drive appears as a drop-down list box already filled with all existing drives. If the Drive property changes, you should change the Path property of the Directory control as well, using the following code:

```
Private Sub Drive1_Change()
'if the drive changes, change the directory path
Dir1.Path = Drive1.Drive
End Sub
```

The Dir directory control automatically displays all the directories or subdirectories of the current drive. You can expand these by clicking them. To see which files are in these directories, change the Path property of the File control to match when the Dir control changes:

```
Private Sub Dir1_Change()
'if the directory changes change the file path, too
File1.Path = Dir1.Path
End Sub
```

The Pattern property of the File control determines which files are displayed. You can set this as design time or run time, like this:

```
File1.Pattern = "*.txt"
```

When you click a file name in the File control, this name appears in the Filename property of the control. The File control also has a MultiSelect property just as the list box does.

In the example program I show the three controls interacting as described. When you click a file name, that name is added to the list box.

PictureBox control

The PictureBox control generally is used to show pictures on a form. It is also one of the few places where a Print statement can be used (the form itself and the printer are the others). You can also use a picture box to group controls just as you can with a frame. If you set the Picture property to some picture that is too big or small for the picture box, setting the Autosize property to True will cause the picture box to expand to the correct size.

Image control

The Image control is much like the picture box but consumes many fewer Windows resources than does a picture box, so it repaints more quickly. It also can be used to display pictures in various formats, but you cannot execute a Print statement on a picture box. If you have a graphic that is too small or large for the form, setting the Stretch property to True will keep the Image control the same size but stretch the picture to fit.

In the CONTROLS.VBP program on the companion disk, you intercept the mouse click event and add a message to the ListBox control.

Timer control

A Timer control can be placed anywhere on a form, but is invisible at execution time. It has two major properties: Interval and Enabled. Set the interval to the tick time in milliseconds. When you set Enabled to True, the timer causes a Timer event at the specified interval.

In the CONTROLS.VBP program, you set the interval to 500 milliseconds (0.5 seconds) and change the color of the square shape each time:

```
Private Sub Timer1_Timer()
'This ticks every 1/2 second
'switch between two colors
If Shape1.FillColor = color1 Then
  Shape1.FillColor = color2
Else
  Shape1.FillColor = color1
End If
End Sub
```

Scroll bars

Scroll bars are automatically part of list boxes and may be part of text boxes in MultiLine mode. However, they can exist by themselves and be used to select any position in any kind of data. You set the

Min and Max properties of a scroll bar and then set the SmallIncrement and LargeIncrement properties to convenient increments in your data. You can intercept the Change event and read the Value property to see where the scroll bar is and take suitable action with the rest of your data display.

In the CONTROLS.VBP program on the companion disk, you see a vertical scroll bar with a min of 1 and a max of 200. The values read are displayed in the list box.

Grid control

The Grid control (not shown in the CONTROLS.VBP program) is a matrix of rows and columns in which you can display data. The relevant properties are shown in Table 2-6.

Table 2-6.

Grid control properties

Rows	Number of rows
Cols	Number of columns
FixedCols	Number of fixed columns
FixedRows	Number of fixed rows
Row	Current row
Col	Current col
Text	Text in current cell (row & col)

The most significant method is AddItem, which adds one to the number or rows. To put text into a grid, set the row and column properties and then set the text property. To read text, set the row and column and read the text property.

The Grid control usually is not part of the default controls loaded with a project. To add it, select Tools/Custom Controls and select the Microsoft Grid Control. You will see an example of using the Grid control in Chapter 10.

Control Arrays

There can be a maximum of 254 controls on a single form, and the more there are, the slower the form repaints. You can getaround this limitation, as well as gain some speed and programming efficiency, by making several controls part of an array.

To make a control array, pick one control and copy it to the Clipboard. Then press CTRL+V for each control you want to add to the form. The first time, you will be asked if you wish to create a control array; answer Yes.

All the elements of a control array utilize the same events, but an additional index parameter is passed to the events so you can determine which of the array members has been activated.

In the CONTROLS.VBP program, the L and P check boxes have been implemented as a control array. The code for the array looks like this:

```
Private Sub TxtOptions_Click(Index As Integer)
'The Locked and Password buttons are
'implemented as a control array to
'illustrate how one is used


Select Case Index
  Case 0          'Locked Button
   If TxtOptions(Index).Value = 1 Then
     Text1.Locked = True
     List1.AddItem "Text is locked"
   Else
     Text1.Locked = False
     List1.AddItem "Text is unlocked"
   End If
  Case 1          'Password button
    If TxtOptions(Index).Value = 1 Then
     Text1.PasswordChar = "*"
     List1.AddItem "Password mode"
    Else
     Text1.PasswordChar = ""
     List1.AddItem "Plain text mode"
    End If
End Select
End Sub
```

The Common Dialog Control

Visual Basic also provides a way to access some of the standard Windows dialog boxes directly. Using the Common Dialog control, you can use the following dialog boxes directly from your program:

- File Open
- Save File As
- Color
- Font
- Printer Setup

To use them, place a Common Dialog control on your form; it will be invisible at run time. Give it a simple name like cDlg. To activate it, use a command button or menu item.

To open a file, set the Filter property to a series of file descriptions and patterns:

```
cDlg.Filter = "Text files|*.txt | Document Files|*.doc"
```

and then execute the ShowOpen method:

```
cDlg.ShowOpen
```

After the dialog box closes, the selected file—including the complete path—will be in the FileName property. If this property is a zero-length string, no file was selected.

The CONTROLS.VBP program brings up the ShowOpen dialog box from the File/Open menu and adds the file name you select to the list box.

Similarly, you can bring up the same dialog box as a Save As dialog box by using the ShowSave method. The other methods are ShowColor, ShowFont, and ShowPrint.

Adding Menus to your Visual Basic Program

If you display any form in your program in design mode and select Menu Editor from the Tools menu, you can easily add a series of menu items to the top of your form. Once you close the Menu Editor, the actual working menus appear on your form. To add a routine to any of these menu items, simply click it to bring up a code window for the item.

In the example program, choosing Open from the File menu brings up the Common Dialog box and choosing Exit calls the Closit_Click event just as clicking the Close button does.

If you have long menus, you can group them with separator bars. To include a separator bar, type a single dash for the caption and give that line any menu name you like.

Navigating Around Your Project in Visual Basic

The simplest way to get around in your program is to ensure that the Project window is always displayed. If it has become hidden, pressing Ctrl+R will bring it to the top. From the Project window, shown in Figure 2-7, you can go to any module and view either its code or its forms.

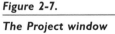

Figure 2-7.

The Project window

Then, from a code window, you can display each control's name in the left combo box and the current methods that can apply to that control in the right combo box. This is shown in Figure 2-8.

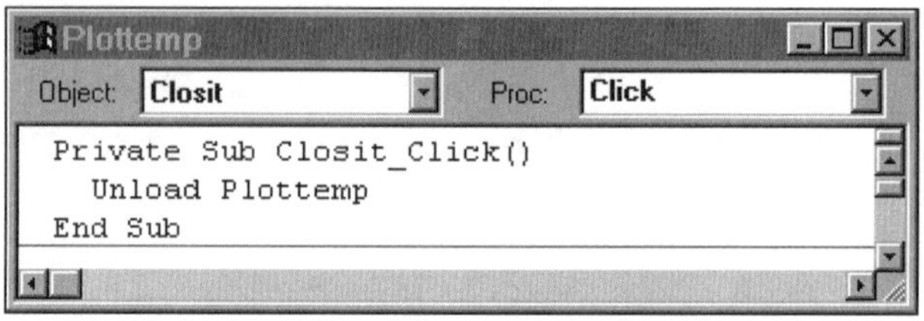

Figure 2-8.

A code window, showing the control name (Closit) in the left combo box and the procedure name (Click) in the right combo box

The Object Browser

You also can look at all the forms and other modules and their subprograms by pressing F2 to bring out the Object Browser as shown in Figure 2-9.

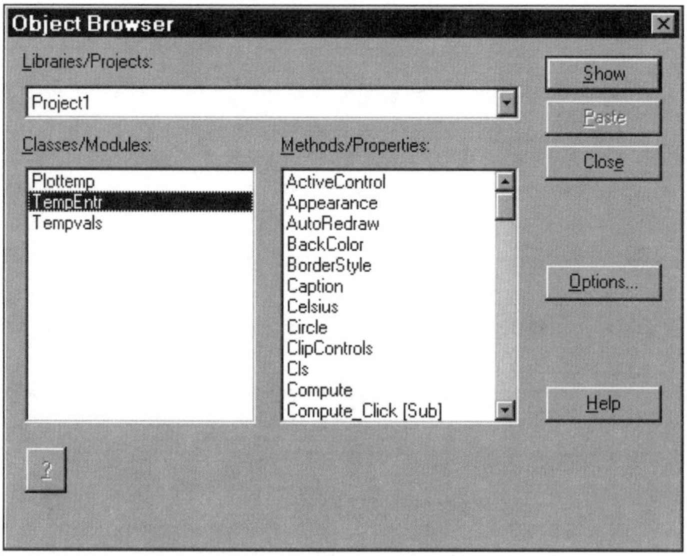

Figure 2-9.

The Object Browser, displaying the methods and properties of the TempEntr form

If you click a form, it shows all possible events, and shows those that are actually in use by putting [Sub] in brackets after the procedure name.

This is of lesser use for forms because of the plethora of controls and events, but as you will see, this feature can be of great value when you have Class modules and OLE object libraries in your program.

3 | Introduction to Object-Oriented Programming

In this chapter, we introduce the concept of objects and how they contain both persistent data and functions or *methods* for operating on that data.

A Simple Rectangle Drawing Program

One main purpose of object-oriented programming is to hide information regarding the details of data manipulation that could lead to errors if they were exposed and easily changed. This should lead to more error-free programs. Lets start with a simple Visual Basic program for drawing a rectangle on a form as shown in Figure 3-1. This program is RECTNGL1.VBP on the companion disk.

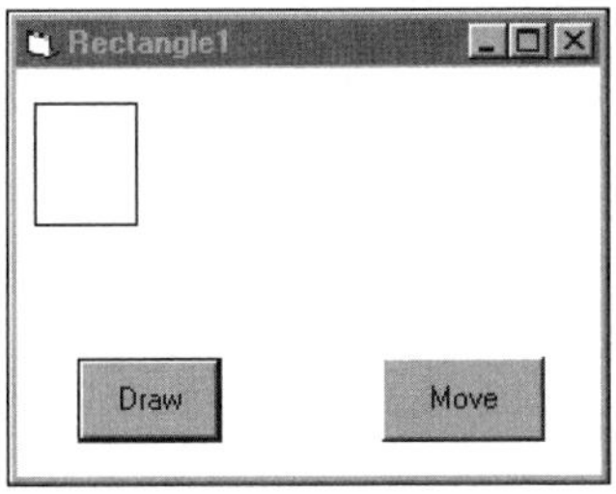

Figure 3-1.

A simple rectangle drawing program

Clicking the Draw button draws a rectangle on the screen and clicking the Move button moves it 100 units in both the x and y directions. The code for this program consists of four variables at the top of the form containing the x, y, and side-length information. When the program is executed, the Form_Load code is executed first, initializing these variables to (100, 200) with sides of 600 and 700.

```
'Rectangle 1 Form
Dim x As Single, y As Single
Dim side1 As Single, side2 As Single
'_____
Private Sub Drawit_Click()
'Draw rectangle at current x,y position
 Line (x, y)-(x + side1, y + side2), , B
End Sub
'_____
Private Sub Form_Load()
'set initial rectangle position and size
 x = 100
 y = 200
 side1 = 600
 side2 = 700
End Sub
'_____
Private Sub Moveit_Click()
'erase old box by drawing in white
 ForeColor = vbWhite
 Call Drawit_Click

'draw in new position in black
  ForeColor = vbBlack
  x = x + 100
  y = y + 100
  Call Drawit_Click
  End Sub
```

When you click Draw, the rectangle is drawn on the form at that location. When you click Move, the routine Moveit_Click changes the drawing color to white, redraws the old rectangle in white by calling the Drawit_Click routine, and then changes the drawing color back to black. It then adds 100 to the x and y coordinates and calls the drawing function again.

Is this object-oriented programming?

First, we have to agree on what we mean by an object. This can be a fairly confusing discussion if you read widely about the topic of object-oriented programs, because everyone seems to have a different definition. Here, an object will simply be considered as a programming unit that has its own data, and as you will see, its own functions for operating on that data.

To a degree, this simple code constitutes a kind of object-oriented programming. If you treat the form as an object, it holds its own data and its own action routines or *methods*. This is called information hiding or *encapsulation*. Other parts of the program can only modify the form's data using its public action routines. However, the form can be a fairly large object and until VB 4, there was no way to introduce simpler objects.

Basic Principles of Object-Oriented Programming

No explanation of object-oriented programming is complete without the three magic incantations: encapsulation, polymorphism, and inheritance.

Encapsulation, as you have just seen, means "information hiding," so that we don't know a lot about how data for a particular object is being manipulated.

Polymorphism means that many objects may have similarly named procedures or *methods*, such as a Move function. Moving a rectangle, a square, or a circle ought to work the same way from the programmer's view, and you needn't understand the differences between Move methods for different kinds of objects.

Inheritance means that more complex objects can be derived from simpler objects. For example, once you finish defining a Rectangle object, you ought to be able to derive a Square object from it without writing much new code.

As our first step into object-oriented programming, we will extract the concept of a rectangle and put it in a separate module. This program is RECTNGL2.VBP on the companion disk.

Making the rectangle a Type

One way to make the rectangle an object of its own is to make a Type definition to contain all the data that belongs to a rectangle, and put this data—along with the functions that operate on a rectangle—in a separate module:

```
'Rectangle Module
Type rect            'rectangle structure
  x As Single        'coordinates
  y As Single
  side1 As Single    'lengths of sides
  side2 As Single
End Type
'_____
```

Continued on next page

Continued from previous page

```
Sub rect_draw(f As Form, r As rect)
'Draw a rectangle on a form
  f.Line (r.x, r.y)-(r.x + r.side1, r.y + r.side2), , B
End Sub
'_____

Sub rect_move(f As Form, r As rect)
'move the rectangle to a new spot
  f.ForeColor = vbWhite 'erase by drawing in white
  Call rect_draw(f, r)
  f.ForeColor = vbBlack
  r.x = r.x + 100            'move coords
  r.y = r.y + 100
  Call rect_draw(f, r)        'draw in black
End Sub
```

Then, the only functions in the form module are those that respond to clicks and manipulate the rectangle functions:

```
'Rectangle form, version 2
Dim r As rect         'rectangle structure
'_____

Private Sub Drawit_Click()
'Draw a rectangle
Call rect_draw(Rectngl2, r)
End Sub
'_____

Private Sub Form_Load()
'initialize rectangle properties
r.x = 100
r.y = 200
r.side1 = 500
r.side2 = 600
End Sub
'_____

Private Sub Moveit_Click()
'Move the rectangle
 Call rect_move(Rectngl2, r)
End Sub
```

This slight separation of the drawing form and the rectangle operations is another step toward making the rectangle into an object. Ideally, you would create a rectangle "black box" that you could tell to "draw yourself," "move yourself," and "change your size," without having any idea how it is being done. Here, of course, the code in the Rectangle module is completely visible and hardly hidden at all. Further, since the draw and move functions are specific to a rectangle, you need to name them rect_draw and rect_move rather than just as draw and move as you might have liked.

A Rectangle Class

One of the most significant features of Visual Basic 4 is the introduction of the class module. To add a class module to your VB program, just select Class Module from the Insert menu. When the module is created, go to its Properties window and change the Name property from Class1 to one appropriate for the new module's class.

A class module is much like a form: its data and procedures are private to that module, but it is possible to make a few of these procedures or *methods* public. In the following Rectangle class, we specify the same data, but make it private to the class module. This code also is given in the RECTNGL3.VBP program on the companion disk.

```
'Rectangle Class
'——These are all private variables——
Dim x As Single
Dim y As Single
Dim side1 As Single
Dim side2 As Single
Dim f As Form
'_____

Public Sub Draw()
'draws rectangle on current form
  f.Line (x, y)-(x + side1, y + side2), , B
End Sub
'_____

Public Sub Move()
  f.ForeColor = vbWhite 'set to white
  Draw           'draw over to erase
  x = x + 100
  y = y + 100
  f.ForeColor = vbBlack 'set to black
  Draw           'and draw new rectangle
End Sub
'_____

Public Sub Setxy(ByVal xpos As Single, ByVal ypos As Single)
 x = xpos
 y = ypos
End Sub
'_____

Public Sub SetSides(ByVal s1 As Single, ByVal s2 As Single)
 side1 = s1
 side2 = s2
End Sub
    '_____

Public Sub SetDrawingSurface(frm As Form)
 Set f = frm    'Note use of Set for an object
End Sub
```

The data values *x*, *y*, *side1*, and *side2* are now private to the class module and cannot be accessed or changed directly from any other module. Instead, you have to use the Setxy, SetSides, and SetDrawingSurface functions to store the values inside the class that you need to draw the rectangle. Then you need only declare an instance of the clsRect class in the main form module and set the values into that instance of the class:

```
'Rectangle drawing module
Dim r As New clsRect
'_____

Private Sub Form_Load()
r.Setxy 100, 200        'set x,y position
r.SetSides 400, 500     'set length of sides
r.SetDrawingSurface rectngl3 'set form to draw on
End Sub
'_____

Private Sub Drawit_Click()
  r.Draw        'draw current rectangle
End Sub
'_____

Private Sub moveit_Click()
  r.Move        'move current rectangle
End Sub
```

Now look at what we've done here. The main module is very simple, and it calls some public methods in the clsRect class. You still have a declaration of that class at the top of the module, just like a global variable, so have you really done anything that significant?

It turns out that in some ways the answer is *yes*. The clsRect module is not just another file with a structure and some functions; it is a real object. Objects are programming abstractions that contain both data and methods. So, rather than call a function that operates on a rectangle, you tell the Rectangle object to *draw itself*. This is profoundly different, because you do not need to know how it does this drawing; in fact, you could have square and Circle objects that have similar Draw methods but totally different implementations.

Further, an object contains the data describing its state, such as its size and position. You could create two different rectangles:

```
Dim r1 As New clsRect, r2 as New clsRect
```

set their size and position:

```
r1.SetSides 400,500
r1.Setxy 40,50
```

```
r2.SetSides 400, 700
r2.Setxy 300,350
```

and tell them to draw themselves:

```
r1.Draw
r2.Draw
```

and you would get two different rectangles drawn on the screen. Each copy or *instance* of the Rectangle object contains its own data. This represents an important distinction in programming jargon. A class describes the data and methods an object will have. If you declare r1 and r2 to be variables of type clsRect, you are declaring *instances* of the class clsRect. These instances are the actual program objects.

You should take particular notice of the New keyword here. Whenever you create an object that you want to use to hold data immediately, you must use the New keyword to tell Visual Basic to reserve space for the internal data.

If, on the other hand, you want to reserve space where you may later assign a copy of an existing object, you omit the New:

```
   Dim pr1 as clsRect
 '...
 Set pr1 = New clsRect  'assign it later
 Set pr1 = GetRect(r) 'or calculate and fetch one
```

C and C++ programmers will recognize this distinction as reserving space for an object versus reserving space for a pointer to an object.

The With statement

If you refer to the same object in a number of successive statements, you can bracket them using a With statement to avoid rewriting the name of the object each time:

```
With r1
   .SetSides 400, 500
   .SetXY 40, 50
End With
```

This has limited applicability because of the awkward dot syntax when you refer to classes within your own project. However, when you refer to the properties of controls, you refer to OLE objects that are separate code modules. Such objects require complex calling sequences under the covers, and VB can generate more efficient code when you bracket all the calls to set a control's properties using a With statement:

```
With Picture1
   .BackColor = vbRed
   .Visible = True
   .Left = 100
End With
```

Object Design

When you start deciding what information an object should contain, you are doing object-oriented design and, as you will see, the best object designs are ones that relate to the physical reality the program will work with. In the case of a rectangle, this is pretty obvious, but in more complex cases, such as accounting or data processing, you need to think through the design process carefully.

For example, in a bookkeeping program, you might have objects such as Orders and Bills at the lowest level. These objects would have dollar amount and shipping cost properties, and payment methods.

Then you might have Customer, Vendor, and Bank Account objects at the next level. These might have Orders and Payments as internal objects and methods.

Then above that you might have Ledger objects showing a view of accounts payable and receivable, and each containing customers, vendors, and bank accounts.

Chapter 5 presents a fairly elaborate object design for you to work through.

Object Review

To review this chapter's points:

- A class module is used to define an object's data and methods or *member functions*.
- Data inside a class usually are private. You can declare data public, but it is preferable to write methods to access it (and do error checking).
- You must write Public functions to access private data.
- You also can have private functions that are used only inside an object.
- An instance of an object is defined with the Dim statement and the New keyword.
- A pointer to an instance of an object can be reserved using Dim without the New keyword.

Information hiding is one of the most significant concepts about classes or objects in VB and most other languages. You don't have to know how an operation will be performed, or whether the object's methods have been rewritten, to make them more efficient. You only have to know the name of the method to use it.

Further, most methods do not have long strings of calling parameters that can lead to errors: Most methods have no parameters at all. Instead, methods operate on the data already inside the object. The concept of persistent data within an object is equal in importance to that of information hiding in VB.

4 | Multiple Form Object-Oriented Programs

Now that you've seen how classes are constructed and how they can have public and private procedures and variables, let's come back to the two-form plotting program discussed in Chapter 2 and explore more effective ways to communicate data between forms.

I noted in Chapter 3 that classes were just like forms, except they had no visual component. The reverse is, of course, also true. Forms can have both public and private methods and variables just as classes can. You will use this feature to solve the problem of passing data between forms by turning one of the forms into an object.

In this case, an object is a form that can store private data and has public methods to access it. As you enter each data point and click Enter, you want to store it in an internal array somewhere. Rather than creating an array in the first form or in a separate module or class, you put the data in the plotting form and create a public subprogram (or method) to store the data points as they are entered. This is illustrated in Figure 4-1.

Figure 4-1.

Communication between the data entry and the data display form

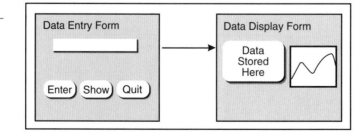

The following code, which also can be found in the TEMPENTR.VBP program on the companion disk, shows a simple data entry routine to respond to the Enter click event.

```
Dim temp_num As Integer'counter to display
'_____
Private Sub enter_Click()
'add data to array
 Dataplot.Add_point (Val(Temper.Text))
 Temper.Text = ""
 temp_num = temp_num + 1              'local counter
 lbcount.Caption = Str$(temp_num) 'display counter
End Sub
```

As you press ENTER or click the Enter button, the value of the number in the text field is obtained and stored in the Dataplot form using the Add_point method. This method is a simple public Sub procedure to add data to an array stored inside the Dataplot "object."

```
Public Sub Add_point(p As Integer)
'add points to array —simple version
  data_count = data_count + 1   'keep count
data_points(data_count) = p   'save data point
End Sub
```

There is, of course, more to this. For example, the Dataplot object needs to initialize its data counter and array. Forms that display data usually insert their initialization inside the Form_Load event. However, you don't load the form to display it until after you have accumulated the data points. There is an earlier event, common to all objects, whether visual or not: the Initialize event. It is here that you set the counter data_count and dimension the array data_points.

```
'Data plotting module
'Private variables
Dim data_count As Integer
Dim data_points() As Integer
Dim data_max As Integer
'_____
'initialize counter, max and array
Private Sub Form_Initialize()
 data_count = 0       'set counter to 0
 data_max = 10        'array maximum
 ReDim data_points(data_max) As Integer
End Sub
```

Now what happens, you may ask, if the user enters 11 or more data points before clicking Show? The program would attempt to store the data outside the bounds of the 10-point array, and this would lead to an error. You allow for this case by checking for whether the number entered has exceeded the bounds of the array data_max. Then use the ReDim Preserve statement to redimension the array to a new maximum without destroying its current contents.

Here is the final version of the Add_Point routine:

```
Public Sub Add_point(p As Integer)
'add points to array
  data_count = data_count + 1
  If data_count > data_max Then 'redim if > 10
    data_max = data_max + 10     'increase size
    ReDim Preserve data_points(data_max) As Integer
  End If
  data_points(data_count) = p    'save data point
End Sub
```

Now you will see that you also can use collections to handle arrays of any size and type.

Collection Objects

A collection is a powerful new data type introduced in Visual Basic 4. Essentially, collections are boundless arrays of objects, where an object can be a number, a class, a form, or any other kind of object used in Visual Basic. While it is most usual that all members of a collection are of the same object type, this is not required by Visual Basic. However, the programming necessary to handle mixed collections of objects is probably more trouble than it is worth.

To use a collection, you declare it with a Dim, Public, or Private statement. You do not have to specify the contents of the collection at the time you declare it, so you can decide at execution time which sort of objects you will insert in it.

```
Private Data_points As New Collection
```

You also can declare the collection class without New and create an instance of the object later, as you can do with any other object type:

```
Private Data_points As Collection
'    :
'    :
' and later ...
Set Data_points = New Collection
```

Collection object methods

The collection has only four methods, which are shown in Table 4-1.

Table 4-1.

Collection object methods

Add	Adds an item to the collection
Item	Returns an item from the collection
Remove	Removes an item from the collection
Count	Returns the number of items in the collection

You can add objects to a collection by specifying them in the Add method:

```
Data_points.Add p
```

and retrieve them by index value:

```
p = Data_points.Item(i)
```

Since the Item method is the Collection object's default method, you also can write this retrieval just as if you were getting a value from an array:

```
p = Data_points(i)      'get item from collection
```

You also can add objects along with a key value in string form:

```
Data_points.Add p, "X-file7g"
```

Then you can locate a particular member of a collection using this key:

```
 p = Data_points.Item "X-file7g"
```

It is important that you don't try to use the same key value for more than one member of the collection, because this will result in a run-time error. Thus, you would probably resist using people's first or last names for key values, since two people can easily have the same first name, last name, or both.

Computer-niks will recognize that these key values represent a "hash-coding" approach that can make location of a single object in a large collection very rapid indeed.

Using a collection in the temperature display program

Now rewrite this same two-form program using a collection inside the DataPlot module. The code is given in the TEMPCOL program on the companion disk. The program becomes much simpler; you declare a collection as private to this module and revise the add_point method to contain only a single line to add the data to the collection:

```
'Data plotting module
'Private collection
Private Data_points As New Collection
'_____
Public Sub Add_point(p As Single)
'add points to collection
  Data_points.Add p    'save data point
End Sub
```

There are no array bounds to check or redimension—this is handled automatically within the Collection object.

Then, the plotting routine is much the same:

```
Private Sub Form_Paint()
Dim i As Integer
'Drawing this during form load is too soon
'and it is never shown
Picture1.PSet (1, Data_points(1))
For i = 2 To Data_points.Count
  Picture1.Line -(i, Data_points(i))
Next i
End Sub
```

In the preceding code, Data_points(i) now refers to an element of a collection rather than a member of an array. Note that the index to items in a collection starts at 1, not 0.

Also note that you have just completely modified the internal workings of the DataPlot module, but because you have not changed the public interface, the Add_point method, you did not need to make any changes in the calling module. This is a critical advantage to encapsulation in object-oriented programming.

Displaying Customer Data

Now consider writing a more complex program which will allow you to:

- Select a customer data file
- Display the customers by name
- Display any customer detail
- Display a list by zip code
- Display a list by state
- Select a customer detail from either the zip code or state lists

This program is CUSTOMER.VBP on the companion disk, and the data file you will open for this and many related examples in this and following chapters is people.add in the DATA folder on the disk.

Your main screen will look like that shown in Figure 4-2.

Figure 4-2.

The customer data display

The group of three controls shown on the left of Figure 4-2 are the Drive, Directory, and File controls, used for selecting a file. To group them together, I placed them inside a Frame control with the caption "Select data file."

For these controls, you must add two lines of code to make a change in one control affect the others:

```
Private Sub Dir1_Change()
'When directory changes, change File1 directory
 File1.Path = Dir1.Path
End Sub
'_____
Private Sub Drive1_Change()
'When drive changes, change Dir1 directory
 Dir1.Path = Drive1.Drive
End Sub
```

Then, to ensure a data file with the .add extension is selected, set the Pattern property of the File1 control when the form is loaded:

```
Private Sub Form_Load()
 File1.Pattern = "*.add" 'Show address files only
End Sub
```

Finally, when you select a .add file by clicking it, that file name is contained in the File1.Filename property, with the complete path in File1.Path. You can achieve a similar effect using the Common

Dialog control functions to select a file, of course, but it would then appear on a different form.

Error checking

This program also provides some simple error checking. The Open button has its Enabled property set to False until you click a file name in the filename window. You also activate the ByZip and ByState buttons when a file has been selected:

```
Private Sub File1_Click()
'activate Open button after file has been selected
 Openit.Enabled = True
 Byzip.Enabled = True
 ByState.Enabled = True
End Sub
```

Similarly, you activate the Details button only when you select a name from the People list:

```
Private Sub People_Click()
  Details.Enabled = True
End Sub
```

The People data file and Customer class

For simplicity, assume that the file people.add is a comma-delimited data file containing a person's first name, last name, address, city, state, zip code, and phone number. Then you can read it in with the standard Basic Input# statement. Finally, you must design a class to hold the data. Surprisingly, you can simply make it one containing a series of strings for these fields:

```
' Class ClsCust
' Variables describing each customer
' as private class members
Private FirstName As String
Private LastName As String
Private Address As String
Private City As String
Private State As String
Private Zip As String
Private Phone As String
```

You have made these class members private, to prevent their accidental access or change by other parts of the program. Then write a series of Get and Set functions to put data into these fields and remove it again:

```
Public Sub SetFirst(fr$)
  FirstName = fr$
End Sub
'_____

Public Function GetFirst() As String
  GetFirst = FirstName
End Sub
```

It is also worth noting that the public functions do not need to relate exactly to the stored private variables. For example, you can create a simple function to return "lastname, firstname" with the following:

```
Public Function GetLastFirst() As String
  GetLastFirst = LastName + ", " + FirstName
End Function
```

The colCust collection

You will store the Customer objects in a Collection object, adding them to the collection one at a time as you read them in. Because there are no real limits on the size of a collection (it is buffered onto disk if necessary) this is an ideal method for containing an unknown amount of data.

You won't make the collection global as you did earlier, with arrays that you had to make accessible from within several forms. Instead, the collection will be private to the main form and will be passed to the other forms using public Set methods for those forms. This gives you even more control over the visibility (and hence the reliability) of the data.

So, start by declaring a private collection in the main Customer form:

```
Dim colCust As New Collection 'customers added here
```

Then you can add data to that collection as you read in each customer from the selected file:

```
Private Sub Openit_Click()
'Open the selected text file
'We assume that it has the format:
'firstname, lastname, address, city, state, zip, phone
Dim f As Integer, s$, file$
Dim i As Integer
Dim cust As clsCust     'pointer to class
f = FreeFile
```

Continued on next page

Continued from previous page

```
file$ = File1.filename      'get selected file
Open Dir1.Path + "\" + file$ For Input As #f
While Not EOF(f)            'read in customers
  Set cust = New clsCust    'make a new customer object
  Input #f, s$
  cust.SetFirst s$          'get first name
  Input #f, s$
  cust.SetLast s$           'get last name
  Input #f, s$
  cust.SetAddress s$        'get address
  Input #f, s$
  cust.SetCity s$           'get city
  Input #f, s$
  cust.SetState s$          'get state
  Input #f, s$
  cust.SetZip s$            'get zip code
  Input #f, s$
  cust.SetPhone s$          'get phone
  colCust.Add cust          'add to collection
Wend
Close #f
```

It is important that you create a new Customer object for each customer you add to the collection:

```
  Set cust = New clsCust     'make a new customer
Input #f, s$
cust.SetFirst s$             'get first name
' :
colCust.add cust
```

If you leave out this step, all members of the collection will contain whatever data you added last. This is because you add only a *pointer to the data* when you add it to a collection; if you just change the contents of the cust object before adding it again, you really are just adding another pointer to the same object.

Now you have loaded the customers into the collection. You can display their names in the list box on the right simply by going through the list and adding them:

```
'Now load the list box
For i = 1 To colCust.Count  'get each member
  People.AddItem colCust(i).GetLastFirst 'add one
Next i
```

You also can use the following alternative syntax:

```
Dim cust As clsCust
For Each cust In colCust
  People.Additem cust.GetLastFirst
Next cust
```

You will see later that the For Each syntax can be significantly faster in large collections.

Showing details

Now you have a list of customers showing in the list box. You turned on the Sorted property of the list box at design time, so the names appear in alphabetical order. Now, if you click one it will activate the Details button:

```
Private Sub People_Click()
  Details.Enabled = True
End Sub
```

You would like to display all the details for the customer you clicked. Because you don't know which customer this is, you must search the list of customers for one that matches the one you clicked. You can do this with the following:

```
Private Sub Details_Click()
 'set Details customer pointer to current customer
 'Since the list box is sorted, we need to find the
 'one that matches
 Dim i As Integer


  i = 1
 While colCust(i).GetLastFirst <> People.Text
  i = i + 1
 Wend
```

Now you want to communicate to the custDetails form which entry in the collection you want to display. Do this by creating a public function in that form to receive a reference to a specific Customer object:

```
Dim cust As clsCust      'empty customer pointer
'_____
Public Sub SetCust(thisCust As clsCust)
  Set cust = thisCust    'set pointer to customer object
End Sub
```

You call this function from the main form and then load and display the details form:

```
custDetails.SetCust colCust(i) 'pass this one in
custDetails.Show vbModal
End Sub
```

Note the argument VbModal to the Show method. This displays the custDetails form as a modal dialog, meaning that no other form can be active until that one is dismissed.

Once the Show method is invoked, the Form_Load event is called for the custDetails form, which now contains a valid reference to a Customer object, and can load the fields to display:

```
Private Sub Form_Load()
 'Load all the fields on the form
    frname.Text = cust.GetFirst
    lname.Text = cust.GetLast
    Address.Text = cust.GetAddress
    City.Text = cust.GetCity
    State.Text = cust.GetState
    Zip.Text = cust.GetZip
    Phone.Text = cust.GetPhone
End Sub
```

The form then is displayed as shown in Figure 4-3.

Figure 4-3.

**The Details form
of the CUSTOMER
example program**

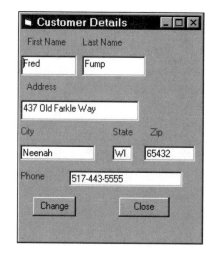

Since all the fields on this form are editable, you could use it to change the stored data. You can close this display box by clicking either Close or Change. If you click Close, the form is unloaded:

```
Private Sub closit_Click()
 Unload custDetails     'exit without changes
End Sub
```

If you click Change, the data fields are changed and stored back in the object, which is now part of a collection. Then, the form is unloaded as before:

```
Private Sub Change_Click()
  'change fields in stored data to edited values
    cust.SetFirst frname.Text
    cust.SetLast lname.Text
    cust.SetAddress lname.Text
    cust.SetCity City.Text
    cust.SetState State.Text
    cust.SetZip Zip.Text
    cust.SetPhone Zip.Text
    Call closit_Click       'and exit
End Sub
```

Displaying lists by state and zip code

So far, you have passed one member of the collection to a new form. You also can pass a reference to the entire collection to another form. This is not the same as *copying* the collection: only a reference (or pointer) to the collection is passed to the new form.

In your design, there are two possible lists you want to show—one sorted by state and one sorted by zip code. You can use the same form for both by providing a flag Byzip_flag to construct the list in either style. Then the click events for the two buttons become nearly the same:

```
Private Sub ByState_Click()
 frmCustList.SetByState
 frmCustList.SetColCust colCust 'pass in reference
 frmCustList.Show    'show by state
End Sub
'_____
Private Sub Byzip_Click()
 frmCustList.SetByZip
 frmCustList.SetColCust colCust 'pass in reference
 frmCustList.Show    'show by zip code
End Sub
```

While I defined two member functions SetByState and SetByZip for mnemonic purposes, they actually operate on the same flag:

```
'—Flag setting in frmCustList form—
Public Sub SetByZip()
  Byzip_flag = True
End Sub


'_____
Public Sub SetByState()
  Byzip_flag = False
End Sub
```

One of these possible displays is shown in Figure 4-4.

Figure 4-4.

Customer list by state, displayed from the CUSTOMER program

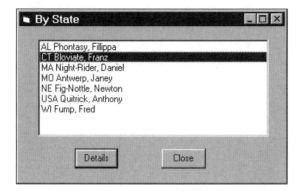

Which display is generated is determined by the ByZip_flag state:

```
Private Function GetZipString(i As Integer) _
                               As String
If Byzip_flag Then
 GetZipString = zipCust(i).GetZip + " " + _
           zipCust(i).GetLastFirst
Else
 GetZipString = zipCust(i).GetState + " " + _
           zipCust(i).GetLastFirst
End If
End Function
```

This is, of course, called during the Form_Load event, which also controls the caption of the form:

```
Private Sub Form_Load()
Dim i As Integer
If Byzip_flag Then
  Caption = "By Zip Code"
Else
  Caption = "By State"
End If
For i = 1 To zipCust.Count
  lstzipcust.AddItem GetZipString(i)
Next i
End Sub
```

Details displayed from the frmCustList form

If you click Details on the frmCustList form, the program will scan through the collection, attempting to match the selected line in the list box. It sends that object to the custDetails form and displays it:

```
Private Sub Details_Click()
Dim i As Integer, found As Boolean
Dim cs$
found = False
i = 1
Do
  cs$ = GetZipString(i)
  found = (lstzipcust.Text = cs$)
  If Not found Then i = i + 1
Loop Until found


If found Then
  custDetails.SetCust zipCust(i)
  custDetails.Show vbModal
End If
End Sub
```

Using Collection Keys to Locate Customers

Another way to store customer data in a collection is to include keyword tags for each member. As long as the keywords are unique, this provides a fairly powerful way to search a collection. In this case, you can easily modify the routine that reads in the customer data to create a key based on the last name and first name:

```
  Input #f, s$
 cust.SetPhone s$            'get phone
 'add to collection using tag
 colCust.Add cust, cust.GetLastFirst
```

Then, you can search for the correct record based on which line is selected in the name list box, which is itself "lastname, firstname." The code shown here is provided in the CUSTTAG program on the companion disk:

```
Private Sub Details_Click()
'set Details customer pointer to current customer


'Use tag to locate customer
 custDetails.SetCust colCust.Item(People.Text)


'pass this one in
 custDetails.Show vbModal
End Sub
```

Timing of Collections vs. Arrays

While the Collection object is considerably more versatile than an array, particularly when you want to locate a member of the collection by name, overall collection manipulations are much slower than those of arrays.

To test the speed of these two data structures, I created a program TIMING, found on the companion disk, that creates either an array or a collection of single precision numbers of selectable size. Since the speed of array handling is related to the number of times the array must be redimensioned, I made the size of the array redimensioning increment variable as well. Table 4-2 reports the speed of building an array and a collection of 50,000 single precision numbers, and the speed of scanning the array to create a sum of its values. All measurements were performed on a 60 megahertz (MHz) Pentium processor in a machine with 16 megabytes (MB) of memory running Windows 95. No other tasks were running.

Table 4-2.

Timing of arrays and collections

Timing (seconds) of Arrays and Collections 50,000 points							
		ReDim Increment			Scanning		
		100	10	1	For i	For Each	No Key
VB 4 16-bit	Array	0.441	0.988	4.55	0.222		
	Collection			57.58	27.03	0.98	952
VB 4 32-bit	Array	0.328	0.39	1.58	0.167		
	Collection			87.58	36.8	1.04	629

The performance characteristics of arrays and collections are very clear: Collections take longer to create. However, once created, you can scan them by index :

```
    For j = 1 to Max
       x = x + col(j).val
   Next j
by key value:
    For j = 1 to Max
       x = x + col(str$(i)).val
   Next j
or using For Each:
    For Each z In Col
       x = x + z.val
   Next z
```

Of these methods, the For Each method is clearly far·superior. If you need to locate a few objects within a collection, storing them using a key will make retrieval very much faster.

Using the Object Browser

When you have class modules in a project, the Object Browser can be significantly more useful. To bring it up, press F2. This displays the panel shown in Figure 4-5.

Figure 4-5.

The Object Browser, showing the methods and properties for the clsCust class

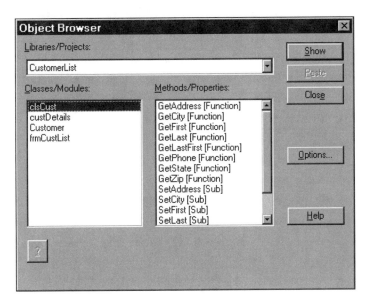

In Figure 4-5, you see a class module selected on the left; the class methods are on the right. You can go directly to a routine by clicking that routine's name.

Summary

In this chapter you have begun to see the real fundamentals of object-oriented programming in Visual Basic. The essence of using a carefully defined public interface to each form and class module gives you far better control of data. Using these public member functions (or methods) you can pass data, or references to data, between forms very efficiently. The Collection object is a powerful tool for grouping objects, where they are numerical arrays, your own classes, or standard objects such as forms.

5 | Object-Oriented Design

Now that you've seen the fundamentals of programming in Visual Basic 4, let's look at how you can utilize it to solve some more substantial programming problems. In this chapter you'll look at how to derive new objects from old ones, at the class Property functions Let and Get, and then carry out a complete design exercise using competitive swimming data for examples.

As noted earlier, object-oriented programming is characterized by encapsulation, polymorphism, and inheritance.

To review: encapsulation, as a first approximation, is simply the information hiding you saw earlier. In addition, you will see in this chapter that you can encapsulate whole classes inside other classes to further reduce the complexity visible to the programmer.

Polymorphism means that the same operation may be applied to different kinds of objects, and each object knows what that method implies for itself. In more deeply object-oriented languages such as C++ and Smalltalk, you can actually redefine the fundamental operators, such as +, -, <, and so on. In Visual Basic, you can redefine methods that apply to particular objects only, such as Move or SetSides.

Inheritance means that more complex objects can be defined using simpler objects as their building blocks. In C++ and Smalltalk, this means that the methods of these base objects can be inherited automatically by the child object. In Visual Basic, you can enclose objects within others, but you must make their methods visible by defining them again in the child object.

The Square Object

The clsRect object you developed in Chapter 3 can be extended and simplified to allow development of a square object clsSquare that has more or less the same methods, but with some simplifications. The program SQUARES on the companion disk contains the following code. Recalling the clsRect object, we find that it has the following variables:

```
'Rectangle Class - private variables
Dim x As Single
Dim y As Single
Dim side1 As Single
Dim side2 As Single
Dim f As Form
```

It also has the following methods:

```
Public Sub Draw()
Public Sub Move()
Public Sub SetXY(ByVal xpos As Single, _
                 ByVal ypos As Single)
Public Sub SetSides(ByVal s1 As Single, _
                 ByVal s2 As Single)
Public Sub SetDrawingSurface(frm As Form)
```

Now, if you want to develop a Square object, you will need the Draw, Move, SetXY, and SetDrawingSurface methods, but you also will need a new SetSide method that sets the length of a single side, because all sides have the same length. You can define the Square class as one that contains an instance of the Rectangle class, and which uses its methods for all the operations it must perform. Thus, the class definition will be:

```
' Class clsSquare
Private side As Single
Private rect As New clsRect
```

The clsSquare class contains the following simple member functions that call the functions of the Rectangle class:

```
Public Sub SetXY(ByVal x As Single, _
                 ByVal y As Single)
 rect.SetXY x, y
End Sub
'_____

Public Sub Move()
  rect.Move
End Sub
'_____
```

Continued on next page

Continued from previous page

```
Public Sub Draw()
  rect.Draw
End Sub
'_____

Public Sub SetDrawingSurface(f As Form)
  rect.SetDrawingSurface f
End Sub
```

It also contains the SetSide method, which calls the SetSides method of the Rectangle class, using the side length for both the rectangle's length and width:

```
Public Sub SetSide(side As Single)
 rect.SetSides side, side
End Sub
```

The calling code in the drawing form simply declares an instance of the clsSquare class, sets the side, position, and form, and runs as the rectangle-drawing program did:

```
Dim Sq As New clsSquare
'_____

Private Sub Form_Load()
  Sq.SetDrawingSurface sqform
  Sq.SetSide 300
  Sq.SetXY 200, 300
End Sub
'_____

Private Sub Form_Paint()
  Sq.Draw
End Sub
'_____

Private Sub Movit_Click()
  Sq.Move
End Sub
'_____

Private Sub Quit_Click()
  End
End Sub
```

This is the approach Visual Basic programmers generally use to simulate object inheritance. For the most part, it is equivalent to true inheritance, except you must redeclare the member functions in the derived (child) classes.

Property Let and Get

In previous examples, you wrote little functions to get and store each value in the class as GetXyz and SetXyz, where you fetch and store a value for the xyz variable. Visual Basic provides special functions called Property functions, which serve a similar purpose. Suppose you wanted to fetch and store the event number. In previous chapters, you would have written:

```
Public Sub SetEventNum(num As integer)
  ev_number = num
End Sub
```

and

```
Public Function GetEventNum() As Integer
  GetEventNum = ev_number
End Function
```

Another way to accomplish this, using the property functions, is to define only *one* function name and specify in two property routines what happens when you fetch the value (Get) and store the value (Let):

```
Property Let EventNum(num As Integer)
  ev_number = num     'store value
End Property


Property Get EventNum() As Integer
  EventNum = ev_number 'fetch value

End Property
```

These are now new properties of the class you created, and you can use them on either side of an equals sign just as if they were native properties:

```
    Set ev = New clsEvents   'create new event
    ev.Eventnumber = Val(GetLine) 'read in number
     ' :
    num = ev.Eventnumber    'get value back
```

One feature (or drawback) of these Property routines is that you must return the same type of value in the Get routine that you stored using the Let routine.

Property Set

The Property Set routine is used to copy references to objects into a class. You use it if you need to make a reference to another specific object within your class. You need this, because each instance of the Swimmer class needs to know about the list of events in the Meet class. You make this information available by copying a reference to clsMeet into each swimmer's data:

```
Private sw_Meet As clsMeet
'_____

Property Set Meetinfo(Mt As clsMeet)
 Set sw_Meet = Mt       'inserts pointer to meet
End Property
```

Then, use this Property function by writing the following code when constructing the table of swimmers:

```
Set sw.Meetinfo= Mt
```

Note that this does not copy the contents of that object into the Swimmer object, but only copies a reference (or pointer) to it.

A Set of Swimming Objects

Now let's put together a more complex series of objects, as you might do in building a real application. You will see quickly that the most useful objects are ones with a close relationship to physical reality. Often, designing object hierarchies is an iterative process: you try several ways before you find the most efficient one. In this exercise, you are going to use an example developed from competitive swimming to illustrate how objects relate to each other.

In competitive swimming, hundreds of thousands of young people throughout the world compete regularly in swim meets that are organized into events by age group—so that only similar swimmers compete against each other—and within each age group, by stroke and distance. Since most pools have only six to eight lanes, these events are broken into *heats*, and swimmers are grouped into these heats by their entry times. In a large meet, each event may have 10 or more heats. Swimmers typically compete in three to six events over the course of a meet, which may extend over two to three days.

In various types of meets, a swimmer may compete in an event only once, or the swimmer might swim in a trial heat for the privilege of competing in one or more final heats held later that day. In addition, should swimmers tie for the last spot in any heat of finals, they may compete in a swim-off as well.

Clearly, such complexity requires computerization, and a number of people have written software to handle these tasks. In this chapter, you will write a prototype program for handling swim meet data. The entire program, called SWIMMEET.VBP, is on the companion disk, along with data from an actual swim meet run on an earlier version of this program. The data file aa94.mt4 is found in the DATA folder.

Object structures

Now you can easily see some types of objects that you might use in designing a data-handling system for a swim meet.

- An event is a set of specifications for a particular swimming event: sex, stroke, distance, age limitations, and slowest and fastest allowed qualifying times.

- A meet contains the meet title, dates, location, and a list of events to be swum.

- A swimmer contains a competitor's name, age, sex, club, plus a list of entries in zero or more events that the swimmer is competing in.

- An entry is a specific swimmer entered in an event. It contains the swimmer's entry (or seed) time, the event in which he or she is entered, and the results of the swimmer's races in this event. A swimmer may have as many as three races for an entry: preliminaries, finals, and in rare cases, a swim-off.

- A race represents the swimmer's time, one or more backup times, whether he or she was disqualified or scratched, and whether the race was official or unofficial. It may contain a list of the splits in that race.

- A split list is a series of times the swimmer records each time he touches the electronic timing pad at one or both ends of the pool during each lap of the race.

These objects are represented schematically in Figure 5-1.

Figure 5-1.

*Relationship
between objects
used in a swim
meet program*

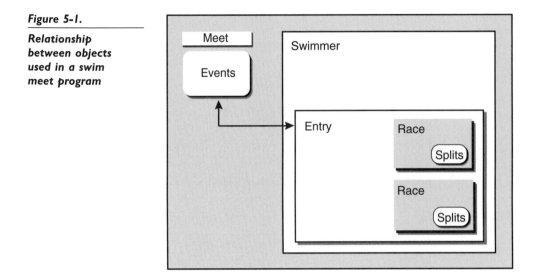

Start by defining an event class, by listing out the data you want
to hold about an event:

```
'Class clsEvents
'Definition of swimming events
Private ev_number As Integer      'event number
Private ev_minage As Integer      'minimum age
Private ev_maxage As Integer      'maximum age
Private ev_distance As Integer    'distance
Private ev_stroke As String       'stroke
Private ev_sex As String          'sex
Private ev_slowcut As Single      'slowest allowed
Private ev_fastcut As Single      'fastest allowed
Private ev_final As Boolean       'true if _
                             'prelims/finals
Private ev_links As String        'list of other
                                  ' combined events
```

Then you need to have Property Let and Get routines to store
and retrieve each of the following values:

```
Property Let Eventnumber(ByVal ev As Integer)
  ev_number = ev
End Property
'_____

Property Let Distance(ByVal d As Integer)
  ev_distance = d
End Property
'_____

Property Get Eventnumber() As Integer
  Eventnumber = ev_number
End Property
```

Continued on next page

```
'_____
Property Get Distance() As Integer
 Distance = ev_distance
End Property
```

The Meet Class

Now that I have defined the parameters for a specific event, you next need to know how the information for a complete meet might be stored. There are a few pieces of information regarding the type, date, and location of the meet, and then there is a list of the events, which you can represent as a collection:

```
'Class clsMeet
'contains description of swim meet
Private MeetName As String      'Name of meet
Private MeetLocation As String  'location
Private Meetdate As Date        'starting date
Private MeetCourse As String    'Yds, Lcm or Scm
Private Sessions As New Collection
Private Events As New Collection
```

You also must write code to read in the details of a meet from a data file. In this case, since you will use data from an actual meet to test the class structure, you know the format of that data file. You need only include a public method ReadMeet to read in the meet data and the collection of events. A fragment of that routine follows:

```
Public Function ReadMeet(path$) As Integer
Dim ev As clsEvents
Dim i As Integer, j As Integer
Dim session As clsSession


 open_file path$       'use local method
MeetName = GetLine            'read meet name
MeetLocation = GetLine      'and location
' :
'Read in events to end of file
'and create a collection of them
 While Not EOF(f)
    Set ev = New clsEvents
    ev.Eventnumber = Val(GetLine)
    ev.sex = GetLine
' ...etc.
```

The Swimmer Class

The Swimmer class comprises data about the swimmer—name, sex, club, and so on—and a collection of the events that swimmer is entered in:

```
'clsSwimmer
'This class describes a single swimmer
'and his entries into meet events
'_____
Private first_name As String     'names
Private last_name As String
Private sw_Initials As String    'initials
Private sw_club As String        'club
Private sw_attached As Boolean
Private sw_birthday As Date      'birthday
Private sw_age As Integer        'age
Private sw_sex As String         'M or F
Private entries As New Collection
Private sw_Meet As clsMeet
'_____
```

The Swimmer class will need the usual complement of Property Let and Get functions to set the preceding values. It also needs a Property Set function to store a reference to the meet, as discussed earlier.

Let's now see how to use this value. When you read in the events that swimmer has entered, you get a record that contains event numbers and times. It does not tell you the characteristics of the event: distance, stroke, and so on. In an ordinary binary record structure, you would have to reserve space for copies of all that information, but in this object-oriented approach, you need only store a reference (pointer) to the description of that event in the Meet event collection. Thus, the swimmer's entries contain references to the events rather than a separate copy of them. You'll use this in the following Entry class.

The Entry and Race classes

The Entry class contains the seed (entry) time, a reference to the event, and information on the three possible races:

```
'Class clsEntry
'Represents a swimmer's entry into as single event
Private Event As clsEvents       'event description
Private Seed_time As Single      'entry time
Public Prelim As New clsRace     'preliminary race
Public Swimoff As New clsRace    'swimoff if tie
Public Final As New clsRace      'final race
Private ent_Points As Single     'points scored
```

The Race class contains the finish time and disqualification status, and a collection of splits:

```
'Class clsRace
'Represents one race in an event
'(events may have prelim, final and swimoff races)
Private Race_Time As Single      'finish time
Private Backup_Time As Single    'backup time
Private splits As Collection     'time after laps
Private race_DQ As Boolean       'True if disqualified
Private race_scratch As Boolean  'True if scratched
Private lane_number As Integer   'lane assigned
Private heat_number As Integer   'heat assigned
Private race_Place As Integer    'place in event
Private swimmers As Collection   'for relays
```

Note that for relay events, the names of those swimming in the relay are represented by another collection of swimmers. You can always fill this last collection with valid data, because all possible swimmers have been entered by the time the relay actually is swum.

Reading in swimmers—a Swimmers class

Now that we have defined the main classes of this application, you need to figure out how to read in and store the list of swimmers. You can do this most simply by putting them into a collection as well. While you could just make this a global collection, you might impose more structure to the program by creating a clsSwmrs class that contains the collection of swimmers:

```
'Class clsSwmrs -
'collects Swimmers entered in meet
Private Swmrs As New Collection
Private path As String
Dim sw_Meet As clsMeet
```

This class has only a few member functions, one to read in the swimmer information and one to prepare lists of entries in a given event. The function for reading in swimmers is shown partially as follows:

```
Public Sub ReadSwimmers(sfile$, efile$)
'Reads in Swimmers from binary file
'   :
'   :
While Not EOF(swfile)
   Get #swfile, , sw            'read in binary record
   Set s = New clsSwimmer       'create new instance
   Set s.Meetinfo = sw_Meet     'copy meet pointer
   s.FirstName = sw.Frname      'read in name
```

Continued on next page

Continued from previous page

```
  s.LastName = sw.Lname
  s.sex = sw.sex              'sex and age
  s.age = sw.age
  s.Birthday = sw.bday        'get birthday
  s.Club = sw.team            'team symbol
  s.Attached = (sw.Attached = 1)    'whether attached
  s.Initials = sw.init        'initials


  'Read in events swimmer is entered in
  Call s.AddEvents(evfile, sw.eventpoint)
  Swmrs.Add s, Str$(i)        'add to collections
Wend
End Sub
```

Note that you put a reference to the meet (and hence its events) in each swimmer instance and that you call the AddEvents member function to read in the events from the associated events binary file. This member function looks like the following:

```
Public Sub AddEvents(ByVal evfile As Integer, _
                     ByVal evpoint As Integer)
Dim ev As ENTRYREC, i As Long
Dim ent As clsEntry


While evpoint > 0
  Get #evfile, evpoint, ev  'read from binary file
  Set ent = New clsEntry 'create class
  If ev.evnum > 0 Then
    Set ent.EventRec = sw_Meet.GetEvent(ev.evnum)
    ent.SeedTime = ev.seed
    ent.Prelim.Time = ev.result
    ent.Prelim.DQ = (ev.result = DQ)
    ent.Final.Time = ev.Final
    ent.Final.DQ = (ev.Final = DQ)
    entries.Add ent, Str$(ev.evnum)
  End If
evpoint = ev.nextpnt 'get next binary event record
Wend
End Sub
```

The critical parts of this function are obtaining a reference to the actual event using the Meet objects GetEvent member functions, and adding this entry to a collection of entries stored as part of the Swimmer object.

The object structure

You now have assembled a fairly elaborate structure of relationships between objects. In an object-oriented tree diagram, you usually put the simplest objects at the top; the more complex objects have arrows pointing from the complex to the simpler. Using this representation, you can diagram an object hierarchy as shown in Figure 5-2.

Figure 5-2.

Class hierarchy of Swimming objects

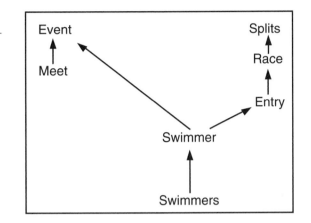

Using the Swimming Objects

Now, let's write a program to read in the data from a meet, display the events in a list box and, when you click an event, cause swimmers entered in that event to be displayed in another list box. The program discussed in this section is the SWIMMEET.VBP program on the companion disk. The data file it operates on is aa95.mt4 and associated files in the DATA folder. The result of the program you design should look like that shown in Figure 5-3.

Figure 5-3.

Result of the SWIMMEET.VBP program

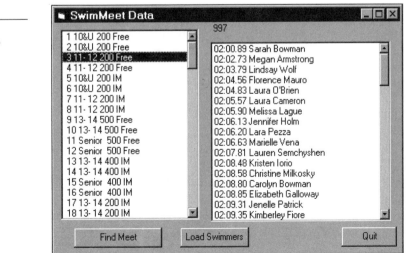

When you click Find Meet, the program displays a file dialog to select the meet directory and file. After you select a meet, the program displays a list of events in the left list box. If you click an event in this list box, the program compiles a list of the swimmers in that event and displays them in the right list box. The list box has its Sorted property set to True, and for this example you will neglect how you can sort and seed the swimmers into lanes from this data.

The form data

The form itself has only a few private data members and functions:

```
Dim Mt As New clsMeet           'Meet data
Dim sw As New clsSwmrs          'Swimmer class
Private path As String          'path to data
Private filename As String      'meet filename
Private swimfile As String      'swimmer filename
Private entryfile As String     'entry filename
```

Displaying the event names

One of the most important features of object-oriented programming is that each object knows how to display its own data. Thus, an Event object has a Name method that translates the internal representation of the age, stroke, and distance into the event names shown in the left list box. In fact, you don't ever have to know what that internal representation is: only that the object knows how to display the data. All you have to do in the Find Meet button click event is:

```
'Read in meet entry file and
'compute swimmer and entry filenames
 Mt.ReadMeet (filename)
 For i = 1 To Mt.EventCount
    Set evt = Mt.GetEvent(i)        'get each event
    evlist.AddItem Str$(i) + evt.Name 'display name
 Next i
```

Reading in meet data

Then, to read in the meet data when you click Load Swimmers you need only call those member functions outlined previously, using the following code:

```
Private Sub Loadswimrs_Click()
 Screen.MousePointer = vbHourglass
 'Read in swimmers and entries
 sw.SetMeet Mt              'pass copy of meet
 Call sw.ReadSwimmers(swimfile, entryfile)
 Screen.MousePointer = vbDefault
End Sub
```

Displaying the swimmers in an event

Finally, if you click an event, the program goes through each swimmer; if they are entered in the event, it adds them to the list box:

```
Private Sub evlist_Click()
 Dim evnum As Integer, i As Integer
 Dim colent As Collection
 Dim ent As clsEntrant


    evnum = evlist.ListIndex + 1 'get event number
    Set colent = sw.GetEntrants(evnum)
    Entrants.Clear
    For Each ent In colent
        Entrants.AddItem ent.GetSeedTime + " " + _
                    ent.Frname + " " + ent.Lname
 Next ent
End Sub
```

Here you see that the member function GetEntrants builds a collection of these entrants into an event, and the For Each loop then loads them into the display. The function GetSeedTime returns the seed time formatted as a string with colons inserted, rather than as a pure numeric representation.

Look at how the GetEntrants function works:

```
Public Function GetEntrants(evnum As Integer) _
                            As Collection
Dim sw As clsSwimmer
Dim Entrants As New Collection
Dim entrant As clsEntrant
Dim Entry As clsEntry
  For Each sw In Swmrs
    If sw.IsEntered(evnum, Entry) Then
      Set entrant = New clsEntrant
      Set entrant.Swimmer = sw
      Set entrant.Entry = Entry
      Entrants.Add entrant
    End If
  Next sw
Set GetEntrants = Entrants
End Function
```

This function is located in the clsSwmrs class. It checks each swimmer in the list and if he or she is entered, creates a new instance of the clsEntrant class and sets the swimmer and entry equal to that swimmer and that entry.

Finally, digging deeper, you find that checking for whether a swimmer is entered entails using the event number as a key and asking for that member of that swimmer's collection of events. The problem is, this only works if that swimmer is indeed entered. If no event in that swimmer's event collection matches the key, an error occurs. You handle this problem using the On Local Error command to exit without adding to the collection:

```
Function IsEntered(evnum As Integer, _
                    ent As clsEntry) As Boolean
'Finds out if swimmer is entered in event
On Local Error GoTo nomatch
  Set ent = entries.Item(Str$(evnum)) 'fetch event
  IsEntered = True      'and set True
isexit:
  Exit Function


'This is the only way to exit if
'this swimmer is NOT entered that event
nomatch:
  IsEntered = False     'set flag
  Resume isexit         'and return to exit
End Function
```

Performance Tuning

You now have designed and implemented a complete object-oriented solution to the handling of swim meet data. However, if you run this program from the companion disk, you will find it rather slow at reading in the 1000 swimmers and 3000 entries that comprise the example meet: it takes more than 25 seconds. At the other extreme, if you write a program to read in the binary records only, you will find it takes one to two seconds to read them in.

The difference, of course, is in how you process the data while you read it in. In this chapter's example, you read each swimmer, copied his or her data into a clsSwimmer object, read in the entries, converted their data, and made a little collection of entries for each swimmer, as well as for the overall collection of swimmers.

To decide how to improve the performance, you need to make some measurements. In the SWIMEET1.VBP program on the companion disk, I inserted the following code:

```
Dim start As Single, finish As Single
start = Timer
' :
finish = Timer
lbtime.Caption= Str$(finish - start)
```

By commenting out parts of the code and running the program, you can obtain a breakdown in the timing of the various program functions.

The breakdown in timing of the various parts of this system are shown in Table 5-1.

Table 5-1.

Timing of the SWIMEET1 program

System Aspect	Seconds
Reading in swimmers	5.3 s
Reading and creating entries	5.6 s
Adding entries to collections	7.5 s
Converting entries to internal representation	6.9 s
TOTAL	25.3 s

It is easy to make one change immediately: you don't convert any entries to their internal representation until you need the data in that form. Thus, you store the data as a binary record inside the clsEntry class, and convert only the event number. This makes the program nearly 7 seconds faster. This version is provided in the SWIMEET1.VBP program.

Beyond that, you would need to consider tradeoffs between the elegance of the data structure and the performance you can obtain. For example, adding elements to collections is very slow, and keeping an array of entries would be quite a bit faster, as discussed in Chapter 4.

Summary

You now have seen how to construct a fairly complex program using object-oriented design principles. You will examine some of these principles further in later chapters.

6 | A File Class and Drag-and-Drop Programming

In this chapter, you'll first build a file class called clsFile, which you will use throughout the remainder of the book. Then, you'll see how you might use that file class in a drag-and-drop program, where each of the visual items represents an object that has a View method.

Making a File Class

One of the more awkward things about Visual Basic is how you read and write to files. You must use a unique file number for each file and ensure you use the correct one if you have several files open. In addition, the syntax for writing to a text file with and without starting a new line is convoluted:

```
Print #f, foo   'writes value of foo and new line
Print #f, foo;  'writes value of foo without new line
```

Furthermore, it is easy to forget to close a file when you are done, if the operation is complex, and leaving a number of files open can eventually reach system limits.

For these reasons, you will create a simple class for handling text file input and output. The file number then can be stored inside the class and the file can be closed automatically when the file class instance is terminated. You also will include some convenientfunctions for extracting the file path and file root name from a complete file name and path.

The private variables in the file class are simple enough:

```
'Class clsFile
'Abstraction of VB files to a class
Private path_name As String
Private file_name As String
Private file_handle As Integer
Private error_val As Integer
```

Then you can write a few simple functions to open and read from files:

```
Public Sub OpenInput(Optional input_file As Variant)
   On Local Error GoTo open_input_err

 'if a file name is specified, copy it in
   If Not IsMissing(input_file) Then
      file_name = input_file
   End If
   file_handle = FreeFile 'get file number
   Open FullName For Input As #file_handle 'open file
open_input_exit:
   Exit Sub


  'if file does not exist, set error and exit
open_input_err:
   error_val = OPEN_FAILED
   Resume open_input_exit
End Sub
```

Note the use of the Optional keyword to indicate that the filename argument is not required. You then can have two possible ways to open files:

```
Dim cFile As New clsFile
cfile.Filename = "Foo.txt"
cFile.OpenInput
```

and

```
cFile.OpenInput("foo.txt")
```

To ensure that the file gets closed properly and the file number released, insert a Close statement in the class terminate routine:

```
Private Sub Class_Terminate()
  Close #file_handle
End Sub
```

Some other routines the file class includes are:

```
Public Function GetLine() As String 'read a whole line
Public Function EndFile() As Boolean'check for end of file
Public Function GetValue() As Variant'get one value
Public Sub CloseFile()        'close the file
Public Function GetChars(n As Long) As String 'get n chars
Public Function Length() as Long 'get length of file
Public Sub OpenOutput(Optional output_file As Variant)
```

You also, of course, would like to write to files open for output. You will design two routines: one that writes to a file without adding a new line, and one that adds a new line with or without any variables. Since you don't know what sort of variables you might want to write, use the Variant type for the arguments in these routines:

```
Public Sub FileWrite(s As Variant)
'write one variable
  Print #file_handle, s;
End Sub
'_____
Public Sub FileWriteln(Optional s As Variant)
'write variable (or not)
'followed by new line characters
 If Not IsMissing(s) Then
   Print #file_handle, s
 Else
   Print #file_handle,
 End If
End Sub
```

Finally, you can localize the manipulation of file names and paths inside the file class:

```
Property Let PathName(ByVal p$)   'set path name
Property Get FullName() As String 'get path+filename
Property Get PathName() As String 'Get path name
Property Let FullName(s$)          'set path+filename
Property Get RootName()           'get root filename
```

You will use these file class routines in the following example, when we take up how to use drag-and-drop in object-oriented programming.

Drag-and-Drop Programming

Drag-and-drop is a simple, visual method for making certain actions within your program obvious to the casual user. It is particularly useful for both the technophobe and for users such as young children, whose mechanical skills don't allow them to double-click the mouse consistently.

Within a program, you can use drag-and-drop functions to indicate which of several actions to perform on any data you can represent visually. In Visual Basic, all visible controls except menus, lines, and shapes allow you to perform drag-and-drop operations, so any control you use to represent your data can be dragged to a new spot on the form.

All controls have a DragMode property, which you can set to 1 or leave as 0. When set to 1, the control's drag mode is set to automatic and will always respond to dragging:

```
Label1.DragMode = 1 'automatic dragging
Label1.DragMode = 0 'manual dragging (default)
```

When set to 0, you must initiate the dragging operation by intercepting a MouseMove or MouseDown event, and deciding if this is a case when your program should allow dragging of that control. If your control represents only one kind of data at all times, then you probably can use the automatic DragMode. If your control may or may not contain data at any given time, you can set the DragMode property when it does contain data. Finally, if your control represents several types of data, such as data contained in a list box or one of the other advanced 32-bit controls, you may want to always leave the drag mode set to 0 and intercept the mouse movement events directly. This is what you will do in the following example.

The Drag method

Every draggable control has a Drag method that allows you to indicate when it is to be dragged. There are three values you can use in this method:

```
Text1.Drag 0 'cancel drag
Text1.Drag 1 'begin drag
Text1.Drag 2 'execute drop
```

You can also use the following symbolic names:

```
Button1.Drag vbCancel     'cancel drag
Button1.Drag vbBeginDrag  'begin drag
Button1.Drag vbEndDrag    'execute drop
```

When you begin dragging a control, an outline of the control moves across the screen. The control itself does *not* move in this operation. If you want to move the actual control, you have to change its Top and Left properties when the drag operation completes. This is fairly unusual and is really done only when building visual control editors.

The DragDrop event

All controls except menus and shapes have a DragDrop event that indicates when some object has been dropped on them. What that control does when you drop something on it depends on the control and how you have programmed it to respond. The receiving control must "know" what sort of control has been dropped on it. In VB terms, these are called *source* and *target* controls. When a DragDrop event occurs, the target control needs to somehow ask the source, "Who are you?" One way to do this is using the TypeOf operator:

```
Private Sub Picture1_DragDrop(Source As Control, _
                            X As Single, Y As Single)
If TypeOf Source Is TextBox Then
  Source.Text = "Dropped Me"
End If
End Sub
```

In object-oriented programming, however, it is preferable that the target control not have to make this sort of decision, and that instead it tell the source object what method to execute.

An Object-Oriented Drag-and-Drop Example

You will now write a program that has two list boxes, which you can drag, and two drop targets: a viewer and a trash can. The program DRAGDROP.VBP on the companion disk looks like that shown in Figure 6-1. It, too, operates on the customer file people.add. It also uses the four .txt files in that folder.

The Find Files button is included so you can change to the folder where the example files are located, which on the companion disk is the DATA folder. Select any file in that folder and close the common file dialog box, and you will see the display illustrated in Figure 6-1.

Figure 6-1.

Drag-and-drop example program

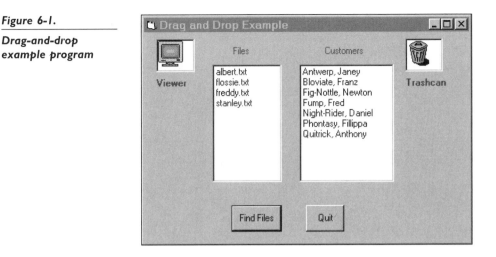

Using the File classes

In the FindFiles routine, you open the common Open File dialog box and select any folder you like. The files with the .txg extension are in the DATA folder; when you dismiss the open dialog box, the program creates a clsFile object and puts the file name in. Then it can extract the path and change to that folder.

```
cdlg.Filter = "Text files |*.txg"
cdlg.ShowOpen
Set cFile = New clsFile        'new file instance
cFile.FullName = cdlg.filename 'get path & filename
ChDir cFile.PathName           'change to that path
```

In a similar fashion, the FindFiles routine identifies the .txg. files one by one and copies them into .txt files using the RootName method to calculate the file name with the new extension:

```
'copy over all the txg files to txt files
file$ = Dir$("*.txg")
While Len(file$) > 0
  cFile.filename = file$     'put in the file
  newfile$ = cFile.RootName + ".txt"'get out the root
  FileCopy file$, newfile 'copy a new version
  file$ = Dir$            'look for next file
Wend
```

Then, it opens the address file and reads it in:

```
Set cFile = New clsFile
cFile.OpenInput ("people.add")
Dim cust As clsCust
   While Not cFile.EndFile                 'read in customers
      Set cust = New clsCust      'make a new customer object
         cust.SetFirst cFile.GetValue        'get first name
         cust.SetLast cFile.GetValue         'get last name
         cust.SetAddress cFile.GetValue      'get address
         cust.SetCity cFile.GetValue         'get city
         cust.SetState cFile.GetValue        'get state
         cust.SetZip cFile.GetValue          'get zip code
         cust.SetPhone cFile.GetValue        'get phone
         colCust.Add cust, cust.GetLastFirst 'add to collection
   Wend
```

The DragDrop interface

The DragDrop display shows a list of files and a list of customers. You can drag a file from the Files list box to the Viewer and have its contents displayed, or you can drag the file to the Trash to delete it. To ensure that you can run this program more than once, it restores these text files from the .txg files each time you restart the program.

In the right Customers list box, you see the familiar list of customers from Chapter 4. However, now you can view the details of a customer by dragging his file to the Viewer, or delete the customer by dragging his file to the Trash—and we've all had customers like that.

Starting a control drag

You are thus going to allow users to drag either a file list box or a customer list box to the Viewer or the Trash. Since these are both list boxes, you want to allow the user to first select one of the items and then to begin the dragging. Thus, you cannot use the automatic DragMode, or you won't be able to select an item first. Instead, insert code in the MouseMove event to see if the mouse is clicked and, if so, initiate the drag operation.

Normally, when you drag a control, you simply set the Drag method to 1. However, if you do this with a list box, you drag the outline of the entire list box, rather than dragging the symbol that might indicate you are dragging only one item from the list box. You can change the DragIcon property to any other icon, however, with the following:

```
FileList.DragIcon = xyz.Picture
```

You could obtain these pictures directly from the icons supplied with Visual Basic, but you would then have to assume that they are always going to be available on any computer you might run the program on. Instead, put the icons you need in a form or control compiled with the program.

Under the 16-bit version of VB, you could create another form called Icons and put a couple of picture boxes on it, and load those picture boxes with the icons you wanted to use. Under the 32-bit version of VB, there is an ImageList control that you can use to contain a group of images. You select a folder icon for the File list box and a person icon for the Customer list box. To use an Image control, select that control from the toolbar and insert one anywhere on a form. It is invisible at run time. Then, click Custom in the Properties window and bring up its Properties window. On the second tab, labeled "Images," you can insert images from the VB icon library as shown in Figure 6-2.

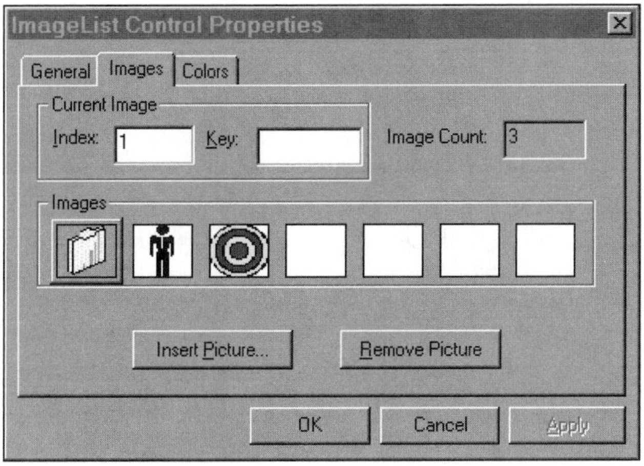

Figure 6-2.

Inserting images in an ImageList control

Then, when you detect a mouse click on button 1, set the Drag method and then set the DragIcon to one of the images in the ImageList:

```
Private Sub FileList_MouseMove(Button As Integer, _
              Shift As Integer, X As Single, Y As Single)
  If (Button And 1) <> 0 Then        'if button 1 down
    FileList.DragIcon = imgs.ListImages(1).Picture
    FileList.Drag 1
  End If
End Sub
```

The DragDrop event

The controls on your form shown as the Viewer and the Trash are both picture boxes. If you drag either list box to either icon, and lift your finger from the mouse button, the source control will have been dropped on the target control, and the target control will execute a DragDrop event.

Now an interesting question arises: How do you know which control has been dropped on the Viewer or on the Trash, so how do you know what action to take? If you drop a File list box element, you would want to display the contents of that file, and if you drop the Customer list box element, you would want to display the Customer Details form.

You *could* use the TypeOf control, except that these are both list boxes, so this would tell you nothing. You also could set a flag within the form to tell you which operation to carry out, and have the Viewer control make the decision based on that flag. A better, more scaleable, and more object-oriented approach is to have the dropped source object execute the correct method on itself.

Remember, one of the main purposes of object-oriented programming is to have an object know all the facts it needs about its own data. A data file object knows to read in and display a data file, and a Customer object knows to display its details. So for our Viewer drag-and-drop event, you really should execute the following View method:

```
Private Sub Viewer_DragDrop(Source As Control, _
                            X As Single, Y As Single)
  DropObject.View
End Sub
```

and, of course for the Trash, we would want to execute a Delete method:

```
Private Sub Trashcan_DragDrop(Source As Control, _
                              X As Single, Y As Single)
  DropObject.Delete
End Sub
```

The preceding methods aren't standard, of course, and they have different effects on the two kinds of objects. But each object does "know" what a View or Delete method should do.

Now, you must figure out how to correlate the Drop object (which is a list box) with the actual Data object you view or delete. These Data objects are members of a collection of Customers of Filenames. To put it another way, the dragged object is a visual control, but the object you want to operate on is a member of a collection somewhere else.

The simplest way to make this correlation is to have a private form variable called DropObject, which you set when the drag of either kind of object begins:

```
Private DropObject as Object
'_____

Private Sub FileList_MouseMove(Button As Integer, _
            Shift As Integer, X As Single, Y As Single)
  If (Button And 1) <> 0 Then
   'Begin Dragging by setting drag icon
    FileList.DragIcon = imgs.ListImages(1).Picture
   'and setting the drop object
    Set DropObject = colTextFiles.Item(FileList.Text)
    FileList.Drag 1
  End If
End Sub
```

The critical statement here is:

```
Set DropObject = colTextFiles.Item(FileList.Text)
```

where colTextFiles is a collection of TextFile objects and the key to the collection is the actual file name. There is a similar statement when you begin dragging a member of the Customer list:

```
Set DropObject = colCust.Item(custlist.Text)
```

The TextFiles class

The TextFiles class is a very simple class that contains a file name and contains View and Delete methods, and ways to set and retrieve the file name:

```
'class clsTextFiles
Private file_name As String
'_____

Public Sub View()
  'View method for class
  FileView.SetFile file_name
  FileView.Show vbModal
End Sub
'_____

Public Sub Delete()
'Delete method for class
Dim ans As Integer
ans = MsgBox("Do you want to delete " + file_name, _
            vbYesNo, "Delete File?")
If ans = vbYes Then
```

Continued on next page

Continued from previous page

```
    Kill filename$
End If
End Sub
'_____

Property Get filename() As String
 filename = file_name
End Property
'_____

Property Let filename(s$)
  file_name = s$
End Property
```

The Customer class

The Customer class is much the same as it was in Chapter 4, except that you add the Deleted flag as well as Delete and View methods. You also add an IsDeleted method to indicate that this particular instance should not be displayed or saved back into the data file.

```
'Class clsCust
'_____

Private FirstName As String
Private LastName As String
Private Address As String
Private City As String
Private State As String
Private Zip As String
Private Phone As String
Private Deleted As Boolean
'_____

Public Sub View()
  custDetails.SetCust Me
  custDetails.Show vbModal
End Sub
'_____

Public Sub Delete()
  Dim ans As Integer
  ans = MsgBox("Delete " + GetLastFirst, vbYesNo, _
                                "Delete customer?")
  If ans = vbYes Then
    Deleted = True
  End If
End Sub
'_____

Public Function IsDeleted() As Boolean
  IsDeleted = Deleted
End Function
```

Note the use of the Me keyword to indicate that particular instance of the Customer class is passed to the CustDetails form for display.

The DragOver event

Any control can intercept a DragOver event when an icon is dragged across it. The usual reason this happens is to change the drag icon to indicate whether the control is a legal target. There are three DragOver states, shown in Table 6-1.

Table 6-1.

DragOver states

vbEnter Just entered the control area
vbOver Moving over the area
vbLeave Moving out of the area

Intercepting a DragOver event is done as follows:

```
Private Sub Viewer_DragOver(Source As Control, _
          X As Single, Y As Single, State As Integer)
Select Case State
  Case vbEnter, vbOver          'Enter, Over
    saved = Val(Source.Tag)     'save index of icon to restore
    Source.DragIcon = imgs.ListImages("Bullseye").Picture
  Case vbLeave             'Leave
    Source.DragIcon = imgs.ListImages(saved).Picture
End Select
End Sub
```

Summary

The DRAGDROP.VBP program on the companion disk uses the clsFile class to read in the customer data and to open and display the data file. It shows that the drag-and-drop methodology can be expanded easily to any number of sources and targets using the object-oriented methods described in this chapter. You also have seen how to build a simple class for file and file name manipulation.

7 | Deriving Classes Using Sheridan's Class Assistant

As you have seen in previous chapters, Visual Basic 4 provides a powerful way to create classes and encapsulate information. However, it does not really provide any way to create new classes derived from an existing one. This is of great importance when you have program code that does most of what you want to accomplish, but under other conditions would need modification to make it do all you wanted.

In an object-oriented environment, however, you simply *derive* a new class from the existing class, and override the methods of the original class with new ones when you need to make a change. This means that you do not modify working code, but rather add to a new class derived from it.

In Visual Basic, you can do this by copying the method names into the new class and having them call the parent class methods in most cases. You then need only write code for the methods you want to change. In a more traditional object-oriented environment, you would not even have to copy the methods from the underlying class into the new one: they would automatically be available. Further, you would be able to specify which of the base class methods would be public in the child class.

Sheridan's Class Assistant

Sheridan Software recently released the Class Assistant product, which allows you to create and derive your own classes, derive classes from standard visual controls, and use specially designed objects to access the Windows programming interfaces.

The Class Assistant program works by keeping the parameters, methods, and properties of your class in a Microsoft Access database, along with a representation of how new classes inherit from existing ones. Then, on request, it generates a .CLS module that renames the methods of the base class to hide them, and exposes the methods of the derived class, which then calls these base class methods for you. You also can override the function of any derived method by inserting code in that new method, just as in other object-oriented environments.

You can create these classes and methods using a Class Designer tool, or you can create them using Visual Basic, and ask the Class Designer to insert them in its database when you are done. This tool even has library check-in and check-out functions so several programmers can work on code without inadvertently changing it simultaneously.

The Rectangle and Square Classes Revisited

Using the Class Assistant, again write a simple program to draw a rectangle and a square on a form. The base Rectangle class contains the following properties and methods:

```
Private x As Single          'position of rectangle
Private y As Single
Private m_xSide As Single     'length of sides
Private m_yside As Single
Private f As Form            'form we will draw on
'_____

Public Property Set DrawingSurface(ByVal NewValue As Object)
  Set f = NewValue
End Property
'_____

Public Property Let xSide(NewValue As Single)
m_xSide = NewValue
End Property
'_____

Public Property Let ySide(NewValue As Single)
 m_yside = NewValue
End Property
'_____
```

Continued on next page

Continued from previous page

```
Public Sub Draw()
 f.Line (x, y)-(x + m_xSide, y + m_yside), , B
End Sub
'_____

Public Sub Move()
 f.ForeColor = vbWhite 'set to white
 Draw                         'draw over to erase
 x = x + 100
 y = y + 100
 f.ForeColor = vbBlack 'black
 Draw
End Sub
'_____

Public Sub SetXY(ByVal xpos As Single, ByVal ypos As Single)
  x = xpos
  y = ypos
End Sub
```

If you design a Square class that inherits from this Rectangle class, you should be able to use every property and method in this class over again, except for setting the length of the sides: there should be only one side length to set.

Using the Class Assistant, specify that the new class should inherit from the Rectangle class and then define a new Side property:

```
Public Property Let Side(NewValue As Single)
  xSide = NewValue
  ySide = NewValue
End Property
```

Then make the xSide and ySide properties private so they can't be accessed from outside the class:

```
Private Property Let xSide(NewValue As Single)
 m_xSide = NewValue
End Property
'_____

Private Property Let ySide(NewValue As Single)
 m_yside = NewValue
End Property
```

Now you have created a derived class. All other properties and methods are copied into the class automatically by the Class Assistant class generator.

The calling program declares an instance of these two classes and sets up their size and position:

```
Private r As New Rectangle
Private s As New Square
'_____
Private Sub Form_Load()
  s.Side = 200
  Set s.DrawingSurface = Me
  Set r.DrawingSurface = Me
  r.xSide = 250
  r.ySide = 400
End Sub
```

Clicking the two Draw buttons draws them:

```
Private Sub DrawRect_Click()
  r.Draw
  r.Move
End Sub
'_____
Private Sub DrawSquare_Click()
  s.Draw
  s.Move
End Sub
```

The code for these classes is provided as DRAWSHAP.VBP on the companion disk.

Creating New Visual Controls

Perhaps the most powerful part of the Class Assistant package is the set of visual controls that have been rewritten so you can create new classes that inherit from these visual controls, and thus modify the behavior of the standard controls: Label, TextBox, ListBox, ComboBox, PictureBox, and option/check state buttons. These controls have been modified to communicate with visual classes, which contain properties and methods that you can modify in derived classes.

For example, a list box always displays all the entries in the same font. However, if you would like to emphasize some members of the list by showing them in bold, you can rewrite the display routine that determines in which font the list box lines are displayed, as shown in Figure 7-1.

Figure 7-1.

The multiple font list box created using Class Assistant

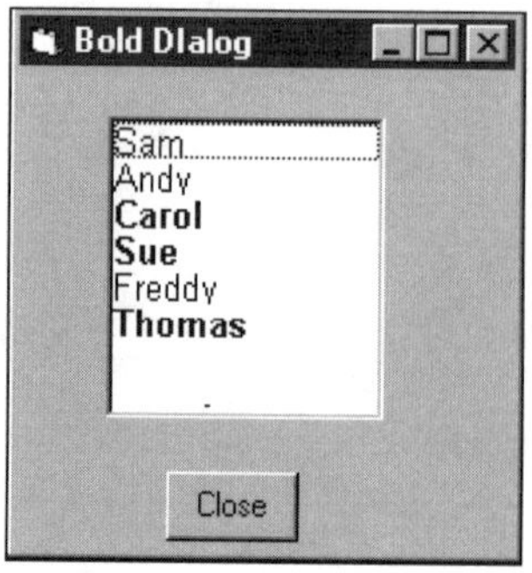

Flag which lines are to be shown in bold by setting the list box Itemdata(i) property to 1 for bold and 0 for normal:

```
Private Sub Form_Load()
  bList.AddItem "Sam"    'Add in the names
  bList.AddItem "Andy"
  bList.AddItem "Carol"
  bList.AddItem "Sue"
  bList.AddItem "Freddy"
  bList.AddItem "Thomas"
  bList.ItemData(2) = 1    'set these to boldface
  bList.ItemData(3) = 1
  bList.ItemData(5) = 1
End Sub
```

Then override the InternalGetText method to set the font for each line:

```
Public Function InternalGetText(ItemID As Long) As String
Dim i As Integer
Dim f As New StdFont
  f.Name = "Arial"    'define font for display
  f.Size = 10
  f.Italic = False
  If m_pCtl.ItemData(ItemID) <> 0 Then
    'check for bold
    f.Bold = True
  Else
    f.Bold = False
  End If
  Set m_pCtl.ItemFont(ItemID) = f 'set font
  InternalGetText = m_pCtl.List(ItemID)
    'return text
End Function
```

The visual classes presented in this chapter provide a simple, but powerful way to derive new visual classes from the standard ones. The code for BLDLIST.VBP is provided on the companion disk. However, since you must have Sheridan's Class Assistant program to run it, you can inspect the program code but can not run it.

8 | Using Advanced Controls in Object-Oriented Programs

In this chapter you will see how to use three of the powerful new visual controls available in Windows 95 in the 32-bit version of VB 4: the ListView, the TreeView, and their associated ImageList control.

Adding a Control to the Toolbox

If you want to use a control in your program, but it does not appear in the toolbox, you can add it by selecting Custom Controls from the Tools menu and scrolling through the list of available custom controls.

In this chapter you will use a command button that allows you to have a picture as well as a caption; this feature is provided by the Sheridan 3D controls that come with Visual Basic. Scroll through the list and select the Sheridan 3D Controls check box. Then click OK.

This will add some new controls to your toolbox, including one called SSCommand. This control has a Picture property that you can set for a Picture button. Further, if you set the caption to blank, the picture will be centered with no text covering it.

The ListView Control

The ListView control provides four possible displays of small lists of data: large icons, small icons, a list box, and a multicolumn report. The icons that the ListView control uses are contained in two ImageList controls, one for large icons and one for small icons.

You will write a program that reads in the same customer list you used in previous chapters, and displays those customers in the ListView. This program, found on the companion disk, is called LISTFORM.VBP. The views will look like those in Figures 8-1 to 8-4.

Figure 8-1.

The Large Icon view

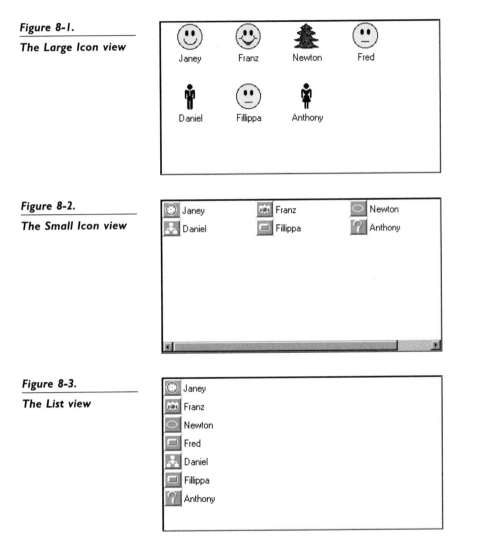

Figure 8-2.

The Small Icon view

Figure 8-3.

The List view

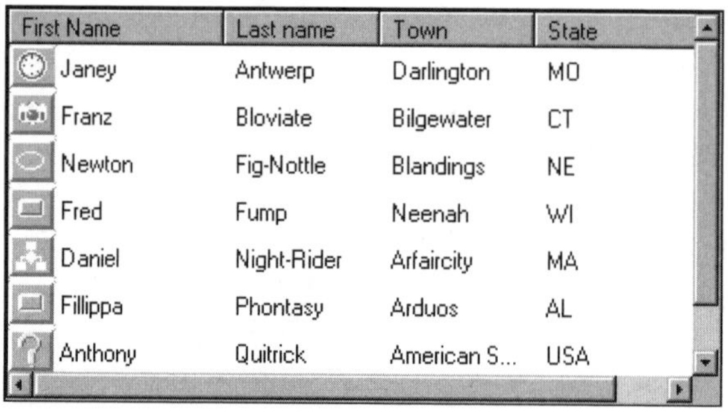

Figure 8-4.

The Report view

First Name	Last name	Town	State
Janey	Antwerp	Darlington	MO
Franz	Bloviate	Bilgewater	CT
Newton	Fig-Nottle	Blandings	NE
Fred	Fump	Neenah	WI
Daniel	Night-Rider	Arfaircity	MA
Fillippa	Phontasy	Arduos	AL
Anthony	Quitrick	American S...	USA

The Report view

Reading in customer data

First use the Open File common dialog box to select the folder containing the file people.add. Then, use the cFile class to read in data, just as you did in the previous chapter, and create a collection of clsCust objects:

```
'Open command file open dialog
cDlg.Filter = "Address files |*.add"
cDlg.filename = ""
cDlg.ShowOpen            'display dialog
If Len(cDlg.filename) > 0 Then  'check for name selected
 Set cfile = New clsFile
 cfile.FullName = cDlg.filename
 ChDir cfile.PathName      'change to spec'd path
 LoadAddresses cfile        'read in customer file
```

Then set up the icons from two ImageList controls:

```
'set up List View icons
  Lvw.Icons = imgs      'large icon images
  Lvw.SmallIcons = smImgs 'small icon images
```

In this case, you defined the large icons to be most of the person-like icons that come with Visual Basic, and the small icons to be anything remotely useful, as shown in Figure 8-5.

Note that each icon can be given a key name and have an index, so you can select an icon to associate with a particular person by name (grin, smile, and so on) and by number.

Figure 8-5.

Icons used with the
ListView control

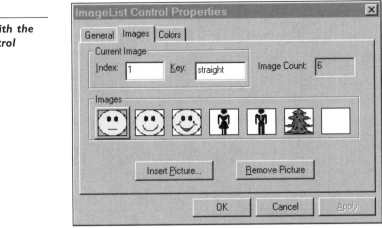

Column headers

A ListView control contains a ColumnHeaders collection, to which you
can add names. When you switch the ListView to Report mode, the
first column is the same as the text you set for the other three modes.
Any remaining columns exist only if you define a column header for
each additional column. You define the headers by adding a name
and a column width to the ListView's ColumnHeaders collection:

```
Sub SetColumns()
 'Set up column headers
 'This creates room for the sub-item arrays
 'used in the report-style view
 Dim w As Integer
 w = Lvw.Width
 Dim clm As ColumnHeader
 Set clm = Lvw.ColumnHeaders.Add(, , "First Name", w / 4)
 Set clm = Lvw.ColumnHeaders.Add(, , "Last name", w / 4)
 Set clm = Lvw.ColumnHeaders.Add(, , "Town", w / 4)
 Set clm = Lvw.ColumnHeaders.Add(, , "State", w / 4)
End Sub
```

The arguments for the ColumnHeaders Add method are:

```
Set cobj = object.Add(index, key, text, width, alignment)
```

As illustrated previously, you can omit the index and key. The
Alignment can have the values 0, 1, or 2 for Left, Right, or Center.

The Add methods provided within the ListView control all are
functions that return a reference to an object as an argument. The
preceding ColumnHeaders Add method returns a reference to a
specific ColumnHeader object. While you don't use this feature here,
you will later when you need the reference to a specific ListItem to
address the subitems for the Report view.

Filling the ListView

The ListView control also contains a ListItems collection. This collection represents the items displayed in the control at run time, when this Add method has the arguments:

```
Object.Add (index, key, text, large_icon, small_icon)
```

The large and small icon arguments are just the indexes into the large and small icon Image lists discussed previously.

Since you already put the customer list into a collection, could most simply add an element for each customer:

```
For Each cust In colCust
  'create list item
  Set ltm = Lvw.ListItems.Add(, , cust.GetFirst, 1, 1)
Next cust
```

List subitems

Each list item contains an array of strings called subitems. Subitems are the text that appears in the remaining columns in Report view mode. The number of these arrays equals the number of column headers you created. You cannot add more subitems than the number of column headers you created minus 1. Thus, a complete routine for adding ListItems also would include adding text for these additional report columns:

```
Dim ltm As ListItem
Dim ic As Integer          'icon number
Dim cust As clsCust
ic = 1                     'rotates through icons
For Each cust In colCust
  'create list item using first name
  Set ltm = Lvw.ListItems.Add(, , cust.GetFirst, ic, ic)
  'additional report columns are subitems
  ltm.SubItems(1) = cust.GetLast  'last name
  ltm.SubItems(2) = cust.GetCity  'city
  ltm.SubItems(3) = cust.GetState 'state
  ic = ic + 1
  If ic > 6 Then ic = 1    'rotate through 6 icons
Next cust
```

ListView sorting

You can specify that a ListView display be sorted by any of the columns of the report view. To do so, set the Sorted property to True and set the SortKey property to the column you want to sort. If you set the SortKey to 0, it sorts the text used in all four views. If you set the key to 1 or higher, it sorts that subitem array element:

```
Lvw.Sorted = True 'sort customers
Lvw.SortKey = 1   'sort on last names
```

Switching between views

In the following final program, you provide a button to launch the File common dialog box, and one to switch between views, as well as a View drop-target and an Exit button (see Figure 8-6).

Figure 8-6.

Display of customers in ListView control

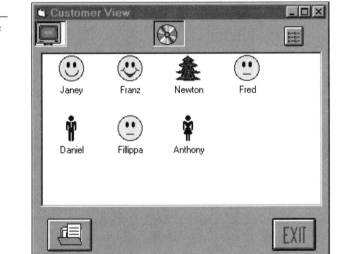

Which view the ListView control displays is determined by the View property, which can take on values from 0 to 3. The chgMode button cycles between the four views:

```
Private Sub chgMode_Click()
Dim v As Integer
'Rotates through 4 possible view styles for list view
 v = Lvw.View        'get current view style
 v = v + 1
 If v > 3 Then v = 0 'reset if >3
Lvw.View = v
End Sub
```

Drag-and-Drop of ListView Controls

Since the ListView control presents series of icons in a window, it is not unusual to use them to drag-and-drop onto other objects. In the program LISTFORM.VBP on the companion disk, you can drag from any of the four views onto the Viewer target. You initiate a drag operation by detecting a mouse click and movement:

```
Private Sub Lvw_MouseMove(Button As Integer, _
            Shift As Integer, X As Single, Y As Single)
Dim lt As ListItems, i As Integer
Dim found As Boolean
  If (Button And 1) <> 0 Then    'in drag?
    Set lt = Lvw.ListItems        'look for selected one
```

You then must discover which list item has been selected. There is no ListIndex property as there was in list boxes, but you can use the SelectedItem property to see which one is selected:

```
Dim ltm As ListItem, key$


  'find the selected item
  Set ltm = Lvw.SelectedItem
```

Then you want to find which Customer object is correlated with that list item. However, since the list items are sorted, you can't do this just by its index position. Instead, calculate the key for that element of the colCust collection by combining the text item (the last name) with the first subitem text (the first name):

```
Dim ltm As ListItem, key$
Set ltm = lt(i)
'compute customer key from list item
'      lastname          + ", " + firstname
key$ = ltm.SubItems(1) + ", " + ltm.Text
'get that object from the collection
Set drop_object = colCust.Item(key$)
```

Start the drag operation by invoking the Drag method and setting the drag icon equal to the icon for that list item:

```
Lvw.DragIcon = Lvw.SelectedItem.CreateDragImage
Lvw.Drag 1
```

That is really all the work, because dropping the object on the Viewer causes it to call the View method for that object, just as before:

```
Private Sub Viewer_DragDrop(Source As Control, _
                            X As Single, Y As Single)
  drop_object.View
End Sub
```

Drag-and-Drop Onto ListView Controls

You also can drag objects onto the icons in a ListView control. If you do this, the ListView control provides the convenient HitTest method to determine whether the object you are dragging is over a specific icon. You then can highlight that icon using the DragHighlight property to give the user feedback on whether he or she is dragging over a legal object.

In the LISTFORM.VBP project, a PictureBox contains a CD icon, which can be dragged over the ListView. Use the DragOver event to discover:

- Whether you are dragging a PictureBox rather than another ListView control.
- Whether the PictureBox is over a ListView icon.

The code looks like this:

```
Private Sub Lvw_DragOver(Source As Control, x As Single,_
                         y As Single, State As Integer)
If TypeOf Source Is PictureBox Then
  Select Case State
    Case vbEnter, vbOver
      Set Lvw.DropHighlight = Lvw.HitTest(x, y)
    Case vbLeave
      Set Lvw.DropHighlight = Nothing
  End Select
End If
End Sub
```

The HitTest method returns a reference to a ListItem object and you can then set its DropHighlight property as part of the same statement. Setting the DropHighlight to Nothing deactivates the property.

In a similar fashion, you can test directly to see if you have dropped the PictureBox on a particular icon, and use this test to view the customer that icon represents:

```
Private Sub Lvw_DragDrop(Source As Control, x As Single,_
                          y As Single)
Dim ltm As ListItem, key$
'see if it was dropped on an icon
Set ltm = Lvw.HitTest(x, y)
If Not (ltm Is Nothing) Then
  key$ = ltm.SubItems(1) + ", " + ltm.Text
  'find that Customer collection member
  Set drop_object = colCust.Item(key$)
  drop_object.View  'and view it
End If
End Sub
```

The HitTest method also is available in the TreeView control discussed next.

Using the TreeView Control

The TreeView control is designed so you can represent a hierarchy of objects visually. These might be directories and subdirectories, projects and students, or chapters and subheads. The tree can include nodes to any convenient depth.

It is common to first display the entire tree with all of the nodes "collapsed," and then allow the user to expand the nodes by double-clicking them. There are two kinds of visual cues you can use to indicate that a node can be expanded: plus and minus signs, and small folder icons. In addition, the control can display lines between the nodes.

As an example of how to use the TreeView control, the TREEFORM.VBP program on the companion disk will read in a specially formatted table of contents file from a few chapters of this book and display it as a tree structure. This file will be a text file with a style tag added to the beginning of each line. The data file is called toc.txt in the DATA folder. A few lines from this data file follow:

```
<Head1>1. We've Come a Long Way Since BASICA
<Head2>Introducing Visual Basic
<Head3>Using If-Then-Else
<Head3>Multiple Decisions with Select Case
<Head2>Looping with While-Wend
<Head3>Looping with Do-Loop Statements
```

Your programming job, then, is to read each line, decide what level it belongs to and whether it is a child of the previous line, the same level as the previous line, or a higher level related to a line before the previous line.

To parse this simple syntax, derive a new class called clsIndexFile, based on the clsFile class. It has many of the same methods, but its GetLine method is a function that returns the line text as an argument, and the level (1, 2, or 3) as the function's return value.

The TreeView control has a number of properties you can set to vary how the display looks. Two of the most important are the Style and LineStyle properties, shown in Tables 8-1 and 8-2.

Table 8-1.

TreeView Style properties

TreeView Style Properties	
0	Text only
1	Images and text
2	Plus/minus and text
3	Plus/minus, images, and text
4	Lines and text
5	Lines, images, and text
6	Lines, plus/minus, and text
7	Lines, plus/minus, images and text

The LineStyle property controls whether the lines between the nodes also include lines between root nodes.

Table 8-2.

TreeView LineStyle properties

TreeView LineStyle Properties	
0	No lines between root nodes
1	Lines between root nodes

Icons used in TreeView

Like the ListView, the TreeView uses an ImageList control to store a collection of images for display with each tree node. While only one ImageList control is used, you can actually assign three images to each node: an Image, an ExpandedImage, and a SelectedImage. Typically the ones you use are those in the \vb32\bitmaps\outline folder. Put an ImageList control on your form and select the Open, Closed, and Leaf bitmaps from the Custom Properties dialog box of its properties page. You will refer to these three icons by name, so be sure to give each of them the key names "Open," "Closed," and "Leaf."

The ImageList control doesn't really provide a good default set of contrasting colors to display these icons in the TreeView, so go to the Colors tab of the Image dialog box and change the Backcolor to dark gray or to Button Shadow.

The TreeView control comprises a collection of Node objects called the Nodes collection. Add elements to the TreeView display by adding to this collection. The Add method adds to the Nodes collection and also returns a reference to the node you just created. You can use this reference to set other properties of that node. The Add method has this syntax (see Table 8-3 for syntax descriptions):

```
Set Tnode = tvw.Add(relative, relation, key, text, image,
    selectedimage)
```

Table 8-3.

Add method syntax descriptions

Expression	Optional or required	Description
relative	opt	The index or key of an existing node
relation	opt	tvwLast: Node placed last tvwNext: Node placed after *relative* tvwPrevious: Node placed before *relative* tvwChild: Node child of node in *relative*
key	opt	Unique string to retrieve node
text	req	Text displayed in node
image	opt	Key or index of image
selectedimage	opt	Key or index of image to display when selected

Table 8-3 shows that you can refer to the icons in the Image list by key name as well as by index.

Now, to actually create a tree list, place a TreeView control on a form, name it tvw, and declare a variable Tnode as type Node. Then read in the data from the index file and assign it as a base node, or a child node:

```
Private Sub BuildTree()
Dim s$
Dim level As Integer, lastlevel As Integer
Dim levelnums(3) As Integer
  tvw.ImageList = Imgs      'set image list
  tvw.Style = 7    'all symbols shown
  tvw.LineStyle = 0      'no lines between root nodes
  Dim Tnode As Node      'Create a tree.
  level = cfile.GetLine(s$) ''get first line
  Set Tnode = tvw.Nodes.Add(, tvwChild, s$, s$, "Closed")
  levelnums(level) = tvw.Nodes.Count
  Tnode.ExpandedImage = "Open"
  lastlevel = level
```

Keep an array of levelnums so you can remember the index of the last node of that level. Then read the file a line at a time, checking whether the level (1, 2, or 3) of that node is less than, equal to, or greater than the last one. If it is greater, it is a child of the previous line. If it is less, it is a peer to the last one of that level. If it is equal, it is another child of the last line of a higher level:

```
While Not cfile.Eof
    level = cfile.GetLine(s$)
    If level = lastlevel Then
      Set Tnode = tvw.Nodes.Add(levelnums(level), _
  tvwLast, , s$, "Closed")
      levelnums(level) = tvw.Nodes.Count
    End If
    If level > lastlevel Then
      Set Tnode = tvw.Nodes.Add(levelnums(lastlevel), _
                        tvwChild, , s$, "Leaf")
      levelnums(level) = tvw.Nodes.Count
    End If
    If level < lastlevel Then
      Set Tnode = tvw.Nodes.Add(levelnums(level), _
                        tvwLast, , s$, "Closed")
      levelnums(level) = tvw.Nodes.Count
    End If
    lastlevel = level
  Wend
```

To keep this example simple, I have not included a final image for the case when a node is selected. However, it is not possible to tell a priori whether a node will have children in advance or whether it is a Leaf. Go through the node collection after you have finished and test the Children property to see if the image for a node should be the Leaf image or the Closed image. If it can be expanded, set the ExpandedImage property as well:

```
For Each Tnode In tvw.Nodes
  If Tnode.Children = 0 Then
    Tnode.Image = "Leaf"
  Else
    Tnode.Image = "Closed"
    Tnode.ExpandedImage = "Open"
  End If
Next Tnode
```

Editing a TreeView display

The TreeView control provides a simple way to allow the user to edit text in a line of the view. If you click the text of a node and then click again, that line becomes editable and is highlighted with a box drawn around it (see Table 8-4). If this is a directory display of files, you could use this to rename files or directories.

Table 8-4.

The LabelEdit property of TreeView control

| lvwAutomatic | 0 | Label edit begins when user clicks the label of a selected node. |
| lvwManual | 1 | Label edit is only allowed if you invoke the StartLabelEdit method. |

You can disable editing by setting the LabelEdit property to 1. If it is set to 0, the default, editing is automatic. If you want to allow editing of a label that has this property set to 1, you must invoke the StartLabelEdit method first.

In either case, when editing finally is allowed, the BeforeLabelEdit event is generated. You can intercept it to take special action if you want.

9 | Writing OLE Servers and Clients

OLE stands for object linking and embedding, and represents Microsoft's method for having a program communicate with other programs. Although OLE's original intent was to have program components that could be combined to make larger programs, OLE primarily has been used to build libraries that many programs can call. Thus, while "embedding objects" was the initial thrust, programmers now view OLE as a convenient way to break large programs into logical parts that may be used by several program components.

Designing and programming OLE objects in languages such as C or C++ is extremely demanding and complicated. However, Visual Basic has encapsulated many of the most useful OLE functions directly into the forms, classes, and the compiler, so that building OLE servers and clients is really quite straightforward.

In-Process and Out-of-Process Servers

OLE servers are program modules that are compiled and loaded independently from your main program, which is referred to as an OLE client. An OLE server can be either an in-process or an out-of-process server, and each type has some advantages.

An in-process server is a dynamic-link library (DLL) loaded by your client program, which runs in the same logical program address space as your program does. Thus, calls to methods within the OLE server can be resolved and executed much more rapidly. These in-process servers can run in the 32-bit Windows 95 or Windows NT environment only, and are not available for users of Windows 3.1.

An out-of-process server is an executable file (.exe) that runs as a separate process in a separate address space from your client program. Calls to functions in out-of-process servers take more time because of the address translation required. Therefore, it is desirable to make fewer calls that pass a number of subroutine arguments, rather than making many calls to Property functions that return one value at a time.

The advantage of out-of-process servers is that since they are separate processes, they can provide a form of multitasking not available directly in Visual Basic. Thus, if you have one or more time-consuming calculations that you want to carry out in the background, this provides an ideal way to prevent that execution time from blocking the responsiveness of your main program.

Out-of-process OLE servers can run in 16-bit (Windows 3.1) environments as well, and are thus ideal for making 16-bit servers built around existing 16-bit libraries, which you can then call from the 32-bit environment.

For example, the Lotus Notes HiTest Visual Basic and C API is a set of 16-bit functions. By wrapping them in a 16-bit VB class library and making a 16-bit out-of-process OLE automation server, you can call these functions from 32-bit Visual Basic and take advantage of multitasking and the advanced 32-bit visual controls.

Creating in-process and out-of-process servers

Once you set up the server program as discussed later, the only difference between the way you create the two kinds of servers is that you select Make EXE File from the File menu to make an out-of process server, and you select Make OLE DLL File to make an in-process DLL server. In the 16-bit version of VB 4, the OLE DLL option does not appear.

Designing an OLE Server Program

OLE servers can contain computational or graphical user interface methods. Some or all of these server methods may be declared as Public and thus available to other programs. When you compile an OLE server, it is automatically registered with the Windows registry so that other programs can find it, and a library of the calling parameters of the public functions is made available so that Visual Basic can ensure that these external functions are being called with the correct number and type of parameters. Thus, there is no need to declare these functions within your program: they are already known when you select that OLE server object to work with your program.

In designing an OLE server, you should decide which functions are most easily separable into a library, and how you divide your program into functions that might be used by various client modules you write now or may write in the future.

In that context, among the simple examples you used earlier, the Customer class stands out as an ideally separable set of operations that any number of your programs could have called from a library.

The Customer Class

Take the same functions for reading and fetching data from the data file people.add that you used previously and put that class into a library. For simplicity of expression, you also will change the Get and Set functions you originally wrote into Property Let and Get functions.

You want to encapsulate the reading of the customer data file in this class, so you'll need to include the clsFile class you wrote earlier. Since this is a generally useful class, you will make it visible outside the library as well.

Nomenclature conventions

Since you will read the customer data into a collection within the OLE server library, you will need another collection-based class to handle this operation.

Microsoft recommends that such collections be named as a plural of the name of the base class. So, name the base class as Customer and the collections class as Customers.

You need two interface functions in the Customers collection class: one to set the file name, one to read in the file:

```
Public Property Let FullName(fn$)
'Sets the path and file name of the
'file to be read in
  cFile.FullName = fn$
End Property
'_____
Public Sub ReadCustomers()
Dim cust As Customer
  cFile.OpenInput      'open the file
  If cFile.ErrorVal = 0 Then'if it opened, read it in
    While Not cFile.EndFile
      Set cust = New Customer    'make a new customer object
      cust.FirstName = cFile.GetValue     'get first name
      cust.LastName = cFile.GetValue      'get last name
      cust.Address = cFile.GetValue       'get address
      cust.City = cFile.GetValue          'get city
```

Continued on next page

Continued from previous page

```
        cust.State = cFile.GetValue          'get state
        cust.Zip = cFile.GetValue            'get zip code
        cust.Phone = cFile.GetValue          'get phone
        Customers.Add cust, cust.LastFirst   'add to collection
     Wend
   cFile.CloseFile
  End If
End Sub
```

Now you also need a way to obtain members of the Customers collection from outside the server, so you can display and use them. Write an Item function with a Variant as argument, which can either be the numerical index or the key to a collection member:

```
Public Property Get Item(ByVal index As Variant) As Customer
If Customers.Count > 0 Then
  Set Item = Customers(index)
Else
  Set Item = Nothing
End If
End Property
```

In addition, you need a way to find out how many customers are in the collection, so wrap the Count function of the collection class and make it available:

```
Public Property Get Count() As Long
  Count = Customers.Count
End Property
```

Adding the Sub Main procedure

Now you have a clsFile class, a Customer class, and a Customers class together in a VB project. How do you make it into an OLE server? First, if you began writing this program in the usual way, you have a Form1 module, which is still there from starting a new project. Remove this form from the module by selecting Remove File from the File menu or right-clicking the Form1 name in the Project window and selecting Remove File.

Now you need to substitute a Basic module having a Sub Main procedure instead. From the VB menu, select New Module from the Insert menu and type Sub Main in the code window that appears. This creates an empty Sub, which doesn't do anything but is required to compile and link an OLE server.

Making the classes visible

Now you need to make these classes visible outside the server. Open a code window into the Customers class and bring up the Properties window by pressing F4 as shown in Figure 9-1.

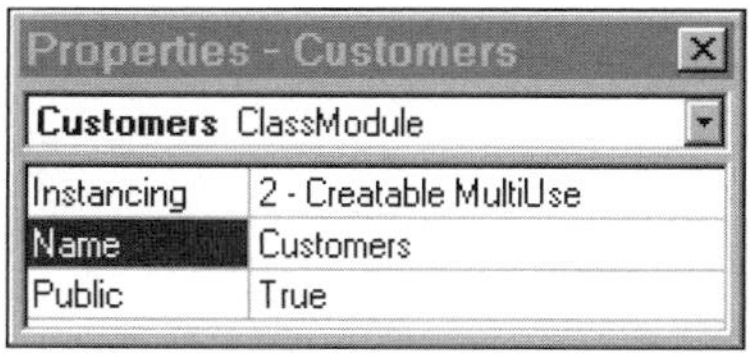

Figure 9-1.

Setting the Instancing property for the Customers class

Set Instancing to Creatable MultiUse and set Public to True as shown in Figure 9-1. Now this class is available publicly and many instances of it can be created from the same server. If you had set Instancing to Creatable SingleUse, a new instance of the server would have to be created for each class instance your programs create. In this case, each server instance would be a separate process and would share time equally with the other instances.

Setting the startup module

Normally the Startup form is the first one created. So far, you removed Form1 and created a module containing an empty Sub Main procedure. To ensure this is the startup module, select Options from the Tools menu and from the Project page, set the parameters as shown in Figure 9-2.

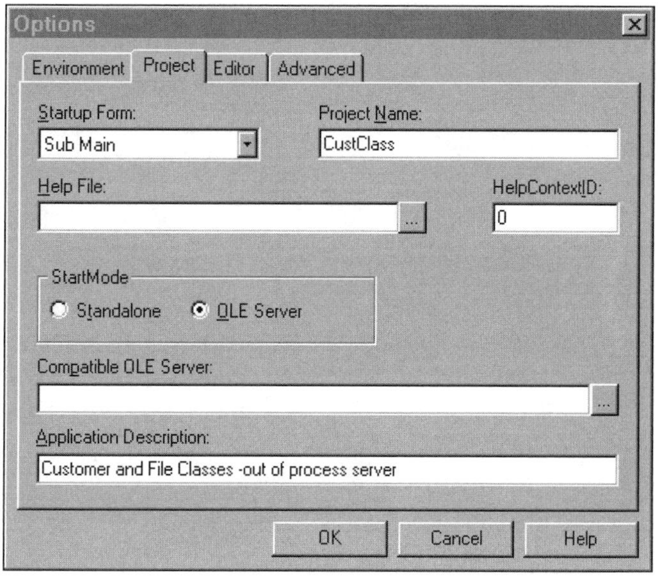

Figure 9-2.

Setting project options for an OLE server

Make sure the Startup form is set to Sub Main. Then make sure that the StartMode is OLE server, and, finally, type a Project Name and Application Description. It is *very important* that you do not leave the Project Name set to Project1, the default, because in many systems there may already be an OLE server with that name, and you will not be able to add another one.

Finally, select Start or press F5 to start the program and verify it has no errors. Then select Make EXE File to compile and register the out-of-process OLE server. Then be sure to save your final project. The program CUSTCLAS.VBP on the companion disk contains the code in this section.

Adding a Description for Each Method

While you develop your server, you can add a few lines describing each function by bringing up the Browser (press F2) and clicking Options as shown in Figure 9-3.

Figure 9-3.

Setting a description of the Count property

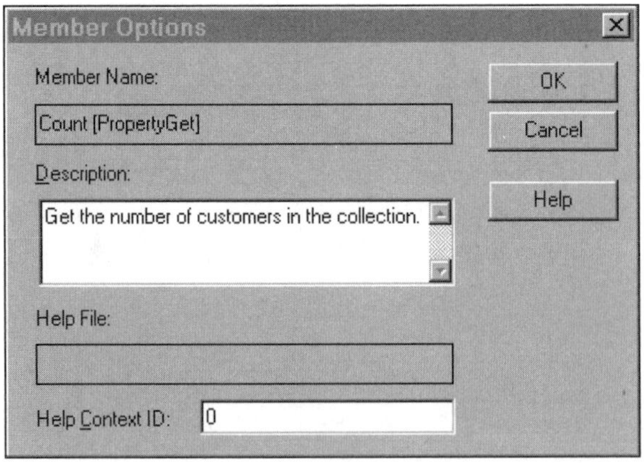

You can enter up to about three lines of text, and have them displayed along with the calling sequence on the main Browser panel.

Testing the OLE Server

Now that you have written what you hope is a working OLE server, how do you test it? The simplest way to test the functions themselves is to make a front-end test form and add these same classes to it as a single non-OLE application. To do this, after making sure you have saved the OLE server code from the preceding project, save the project again as CUSTTEST.VBP and add a form to the project containing a Common Dialog control, a label, two command buttons, and a horizontal Scroll Bar control as shown in Figure 9-4.

Figure 9-4.

*Design of the
Customer view*

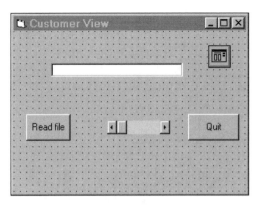

The ReadFile command button will call the common Open File dialog box, and allow you to find and select the people.add customer address file. Then it calls the Customers.ReadCustomer method to read in the data:

```
Private Sub Readfile_Click()

'Set up file filter and call common dialog
cDlg.Filter = "Customers |*.add"
cDlg.ShowOpen


If Len(cDlg.filename) > 0 Then
  'read in customers
  Custs.FullName = cDlg.filename     'give it the filename
  Custs.ReadCustomers        'read in the file
  Set cust = Custs.Item(1)        'put first name
  lbname.Caption = cust.LastFirst  'in label caption
```

Next set up the boundaries for the horizontal scroll bar:

```
  'set scroll bar to represent extents of collection
  HScroll1.Max = Custs.Count
  HScroll1.Min = 1
  HScroll1.SmallChange = 1
  HScroll1.LargeChange = 3
  HScroll1.Enabled = True    'turn on scroll bar
  Readfile.Enabled = False  'disable Read file button
End If
```

Then each time you click the scroll bar, a new name is displayed:

```
Private Sub HScroll1_Change()
 'get index of next customer
 'from scroll bar position
 Set cust = Custs.Item(HScroll1.Value)
 lbname.Caption = cust.LastFirst 'display that name
End Sub
```

This is shown in Figure 9-5.

Figure 9-5.

The CUSTTEST program running in client/server mode

The program is on the companion disk as CUSTTEST.VBP.

If you find and correct any errors in the classes when you run your test program, go back and recompile the OLE server as well.

Building a Test OLE Client

Now that you have written a single program that correctly exercises the functions of the classes with test data, change this to be an OLE client to the out-of-process server you just compiled.

Create a new project and add just the Customer View form to it. The program OUTPTEST.VBP on the companion disk illustrates these functions. Then select References from the Tools menu. You should find that one of the available OLE servers is the one you just created, usually at the bottom of the list. Check that server and click OK, as shown in Figure 9-6.

That's all there is to it. You have compiled the server, which registered it in the Windows registry, and selected it from the References window. Now you should be able to run this new program directly. Try it.

Figure 9-6.

The Tools/References display, showing the new out-of-process server

The Object Browser

You might be surprised to discover that the Object Browser displayed when you press F2 can show the methods and argument for any OLE server. These are kept in a TypeLib which is stored with the OLE control and is available for type checking. The comments you entered regarding each function are also displayed as shown in Figure 9-7.

Note that both the calling sequence and the comments you entered are displayed.

Figure 9-7.

The Object Browser, showing the Count method, its calling sequence, and comment

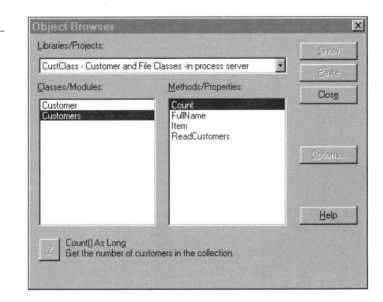

Creating an In-Process Server

In-process servers are DLLs and can only be used in 32-bit environments such as Windows 95 and Windows NT, and they will not work in Windows 3.1. To create one, reload the CUSTCLAS.VBP program on the companion disk. Choose Options from the Tools menu and change the comment on the Project page to "Customer and File Classes—In-Process Server." Then instead of selecting Make EXE File from the File menu, select Make OLE DLL File. This will make the .dll and register it for you. This is the INPTEST program on the companion disk.

To test the in-process server, create a new project with the same main form, but select the in-process server from the References window, and run the program.

Figure 9-8.

The MISSING and new customer servers

Errors in Finding OLE Servers

Sometimes when loading or running a program that you have been testing, along with making changes in the OLE server code you will get a message that the program can't find or load the server. If you look at the References window, you will find that the server is marked as "MISSING" as shown in Figure 9-8.

However, if you clear the missing server's check box and scroll to the bottom of the list, you usually will find that a newer version of that server now exists. If they have the same name, you may have to close and reopen the References window to see the new one displayed. Select the new one and close the dialog box, and your program now will work correctly.

Optimizing Passing and Fetching Parameters

When you write a program as a single executable, you consider using the ByVal keyword primarily when you want to ensure that the called procedure cannot change the calling parameters. You omit the keyword or use the default ByRef keyword if you want to pass a pointer to a variable, rather than copying the variable (or array) itself. The same philosophy applies to in-process OLE servers, because they share the same address space with the calling program.

However, the situation is reversed for out-of-process servers, because they do not share the same address space. In fact, VB and Windows copy all the data from one process to another, if you specify ByRef and copy it back again. If you specify ByVal, the data are only copied once. Thus, if you have a large data array, you should specify ByRef for in-process servers but ByVal for out-of-process servers.

10 | Manipulating Databases in Visual Basic

A database is a set of tables kept in a file or group of files. Relational databases keep indexes to a series of tables so that they can be viewed and combined quite rapidly. The native format for databases created by or read by Visual Basic is, of course, Microsoft Access, but using a library of functions called the Jet Engine, VB also can access data in Btrieve, FoxPro, dBase, Paradox databases, Lotus 1-2-3 and Microsoft Excel spreadsheets, and text files.

There are several ways to access this data. The simplest is by using the data-aware controls that can be attached to the Data control; the more powerful programmatic method uses the data access objects library to manipulate the database contents.

Data-Aware Controls

Data-aware controls, or *bound data controls,* allow you to connect various standard controls to the Data control, and connect the Data control to a database, providing a simple code-free way of viewing and changing database fields.

These VB controls allow you to view and change database fields:

- TextBox
- CheckBox
- Image
- Label

- PictureBox
- ListBox
- ComboBox
- OLE Container
- DBList
- DBCombo
- DBGrid

In each case, you use these by putting an invisible Data control on your form and connecting the data-aware control to the Data control.

Using the DBGrid

Let's take a simple example. You'll open a new project and put a Data control and a DBGrid control on the form. Stretch out the DBGrid control so that you can see the label in the middle. Name the control dControl as shown in Figure 10-1.

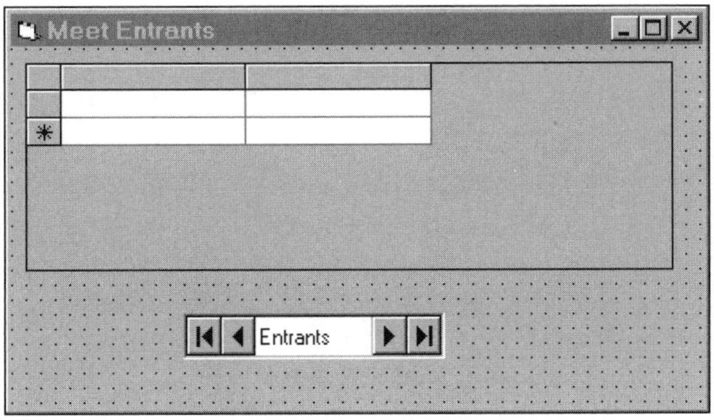

Figure 10-1.

Putting a Data control on the form along with the DBGrid control

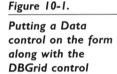

Now connect the Data control to a database by setting some properties. Throughout this chapter, you will use data from the 1995 Special Olympics World Games, which was originally kept in a FoxPro database and was converted to a Microsoft Access database when most of the entries were completed. You'll access both data types in this chapter's examples.

Select the Data control and display its Properties window. Set the Connect property to Access databases as shown in Figure 10-2.

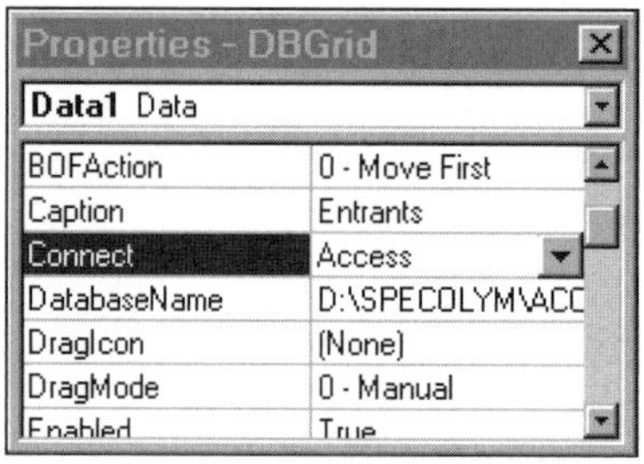

Figure 10-2.

Setting the Connect property to Access

Set the DatabaseName property to the Access file name you will view. On the companion disk, this data file is called gamemgmt.mdb and is in the DATA folder. Click the RecordSource property. Scrolling down will reveal a list of all the tables in the database. Select the Competitor table as shown in Figure 10.3.

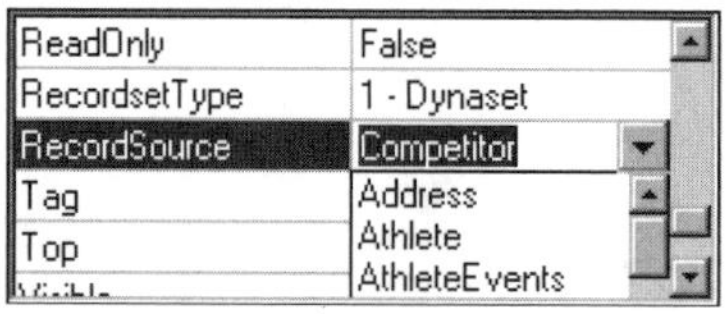

Figure 10-3.

Selecting the Competitor table as the RecordSource

Select the DBGrid and set its DataSource property to the Data control's name—dControl—as shown in Figure 10-4.

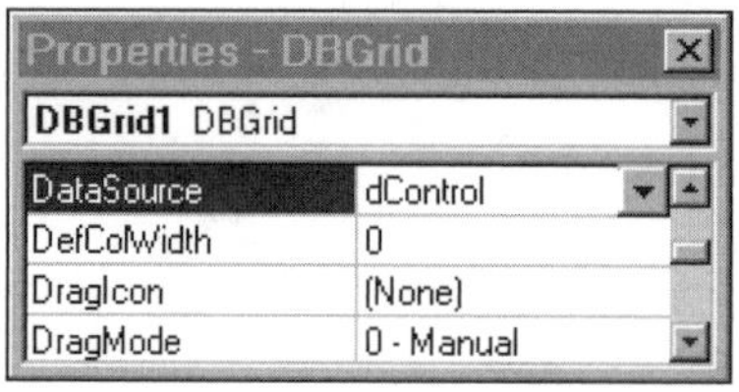

Figure 10-4.

Setting the DataSource to dControl

You have established the program by setting just a couple of control properties. The DBGrid now will display all the columns and rows of the Competitor table. Start the program by pressing F5. You should see the display shown in Figure 10-5.

You can use the Data control or the DBGrid scroll bar to scroll through the table.

The DBGrid is unique in that you can edit any cell of the table. These edits are also data-aware, and you can change the underlying database in this simple fashion. If you want only to read and display the data and do not want to change it, set the ReadOnly property of the Data control to True. This program is called DBGRID.VBP on the companion disk.

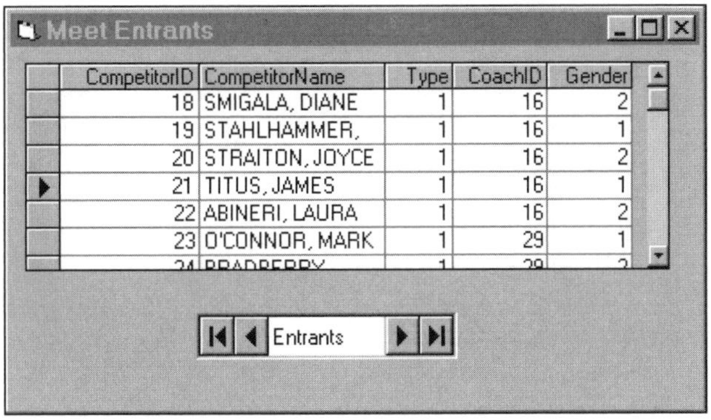

Figure 10-5.

The Data control filled from a database

Selecting data to display using SQL

As you can see, the preceding name list is ordered by CompetitorID and so is not in any useful order. The program would be far more useful if you sorted the names or used other criteria to select which ones to display. You can do this by changing the RecordSource property from a table name to a Structured Query Language (SQL) statement. SQL (often pronounced "sequel") is an industry-standard query language for obtaining data from databases. In this case, the SQL statement is quite simple: you need to select the same columns, but order them by name as shown in Figure 10-6. The SQL statement is:

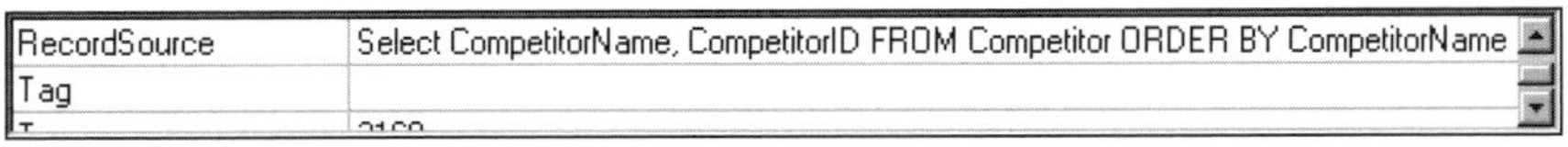

Figure 10-6.

Setting an SQL statement in the RecordSource

```
Select CompetitorName, CompetitorID, FROM Competitor _
    ORDER BY CompetitorName
```

The SQL language is described in some detail in the Visual Basic Professional Features guide, as well as in any number of books on the subject referenced there and in the sample database provided with VB. Thus, I will not cover its syntax here.

Once we have run the program and executed the SQL in the RecordSource, the final display is shown in Figure 10-7. This program is DBGRID1.VBP on the companion disk.

Writing Programs to Access Databases

While you can do a fair amount of filtering and display, and modify databases fairly quickly using the bound Data controls, you have only limited ways of acting on or converting data based on user actions or multiple data inputs. In recent years, the concept of a *data warehouse* has grown in popularity. With it, you use various tools to make data from different sources available in a common format, so your users can compare the data and prepare new databases or tables from the data even though it is in different formats and comes from different sources.

To write programs that access databases, you must have included a reference to the Microsoft Data Access Objects (DAO) libraries. There are two separate versions of this database engine: version 2.5 for 16-bit programming and version 3.0 for 32-bit programming. Make sure you select the correct one for the version of the compiler you use.

Operations on databases are encapsulated into Database objects and various types of Recordset objects constructed from them. For the most part, it doesn't matter which kind of database you access: the operations are abstracted to a level such that the operations are the same for all the supported database formats.

While it is possible to create and maintain databases directly using Visual Basic, it is far more common to access one or more databases that were produced by standard applications, using Visual Basic to provide a friendlier interface to navigate through the data. In this chapter you will deal exclusively with the problem of accessing data from existing databases.

The Workspace and Database Objects

While database access within Visual Basic always has been more or less object-oriented, even in previous versions, the objects are much more clearly delineated in VB 4. Some of the major objects are shown schematically in Table 10-1.

Table 10-1.

Database objects in VB 4

DBEngine	The Microsoft Jet database engine
Workspace	A working area for a single job
Database	A single database
TableDef	A table in the current database
Recordset	Rows of data from one or more tables
QueryDef	Stored SQL query
Field	A column of data
Index	A collection of pointers that allow you to access sorted data

Now, to begin accessing the data in a database, select the 0th workspace and pass the file name to the OpenDatabase method (the OpenDatabase variables are described in Table 10-2):

```
Set ws = DBEngine.Workspaces(0)
Set db = ws.OpenDatabase(dbFileName, Excl, Rdonly, cString)
```

Table 10-2.

OpenDatabase variables

Variable	Description
dbFileName	The database path and file name
Excl	True if opened exclusively
Rdonly	True if Read only
cString	The database type as a connect string shown in Table 10-3

Note that the databases are described by a connect string, which always must end in a semicolon, as shown in Table 10-3.

Table 10-3.

Database connect strings

Database type	Connect string	Filename format
Access	";"	"drive:\path\filename.MDB"
dBASE III	"dBASE III;"	"drive:\path"
dBASE IV	"dBASE IV;"	"drive:\path"
Paradox 3.*x*	"Paradox 3.x;"	"drive:\path"
Paradox 4.*x*	"Paradox 4.x;"	"drive:\path"
Btrieve	"Btrieve;"	"drive:\path\filename.DDF"
FoxPro 2.0	"FoxPro 2.0;"	"drive:\path"

Continued on next page

FoxPro 2.5	"FoxPro 2.5;"	"drive:\path"
FoxPro 2.6	"FoxPro 2.6;"	"drive:\path"
Excel 3.0	"Excel 3.0;"	"drive:\path\filename.XLS"
Excel 4.0	"Excel 4.0;"	"drive:\path\filename.XLS"
Excel 5.0	"Excel 5.0;"	"drive:\path\filename.XLS"

Once you have opened the database, the operations you can perform on it are virtually identical regardless of which format the data is stored in.

As may be apparent from the prior schematic, each database is made up of Tabledef objects, which in turn are made up of Field objects. More to the point, each database contains a Tabledefs collection of Tabledef objects, and each Tabledef object contains a Fields collection of Field objects. Thus, you easily can open a database and enumerate its existing tables:

```
Dim ws As WorkSpace
Dim db As Database
Dim tb As TableDef
Set ws = DBEngine.Workspaces(0)
Set db = ws.OpenDatabase(dbfilename, False, False, dbtype)


'List out names of Tabeldef objects
For Each tb In db.TableDefs
    List1.AddItem tb.Name
Next tb
```

Then, when you click any Tabledef name in the List1 list box, the program can use this name as a key to obtain the Fields collection for that table:

```
Private Sub List1_Click()
'List out fields of selected Tabledef
Dim tb As TableDef
Dim fld As Field


List2.Clear
Set tb = db.TableDefs(List1.Text) 'use name as key
For Each fld In tb.Fields
  List2.AddItem fld.Name
Next fld
End Sub
```

Building Recordsets

A Recordset object is a set of rows of data extracted from the database. You can extract all the data in one or more tables or some subset of that data. There are three types of recordsets: table, dynaset, and snapshot.

A table recordset is a single table in the current database. A dynaset (for dynamic dataset) recordset is usually one constructed as the result of some query, and may contain data from one or more local tables or included data from attached tables from other databases.

Both the dynaset and table recordsets allow you to read and modify the data in the database. Any change you make in either of these Recordset object types is reflected automatically in the underlying database.

A snapshot recordset is a picture of how the data appeared at a particular moment. You can't change this data or affect the underlying database from this kind of recordset. Snapshots are usually used only to read data.

Opening a recordset

If you want to list the contents of a field for the entire database, you must construct a recordset containing that table and field:

```
Private Sub List2_Click()
Dim rec As Recordset


'open recordset from table named in List1
Set rec = db.OpenRecordset(List1.Text, dbOpenTable)


'list out field whose name is selected in List2
Do Until rec.EOF
  List3.AddItem rec(List2.Text)
  rec.MoveNext
Loop
rec.Close
End Sub
```

In this case, the dbOpenTable constant specified that you want to open a table recordset. The other constants are dbOpenDynaset and dbOpenSnapshot.

Note that there is no particular reason to assume that these tables, fields, and data will be sorted, so you set the Sorted property of each list box. The result is shown in Figure 10-8. This code is given in the program ENUMRATE.VBP on the companion disk.

You also could have used the ORDER BY verb in an SQL statement to achieve this sorting.

Recordsets from queries

More commonly, you construct recordsets from SQL queries so that the records you include are those that specifically interest you. Then, instead of a table name, you include the SQL query. In the following example, you pick out only the competitors having a last name starting with B. Note that this is not a whole table but a new dynaset structure.

```
Private Sub SQL_Click()
Dim rec As Recordset, sqltext$
sqltext$ = _
  "SELECT * FROM Competitor WHERE [CompetitorName] Like 'B*'"
Set rec = db.OpenRecordset(sqltext$, dbOpenDynaset)
Do Until rec.EOF
  List3.AddItem rec("CompetitorName")
  rec.MoveNext
Loop
rec.Close
End Sub
```

Use the MoveNext method to move through the recordset until the EOF property becomes True. Other navigational methods include:

- MoveFirst
- MoveLast
- MovePrevious

More Complex Queries

For your final database example, you will revisit a problem you solved during the entry processing for the 1995 Special Olympics World Games. The original entries from teams were received on paper and entered into a FoxPro database, and snapshots of these entries were available regularly as they trickled in from around the world. However, the goal was to convert to a newer and more complex database structure—based on Microsoft Access—near the end of the entry process.

The problem was to extract the aquatics events from these databases to analyze the size of the entry to determine the optimum event order and how long each session would take: there were six different sessions scheduled over a seven-day period. Further, you had to place this data into a swim meet management program much like the one developed in Chapter 5, so you could print out information sheets and enter results during the meet.

Both the FoxPro and Access databases contained data from 19 different sports. While there were marked differences, the main questions to be answered were:

- Which athletes are entered in aquatic events?
- Which events are they entered in and at what seed times?

Thus for the two kinds of databases, you need to find all the athletes, and find which were entered in aquatic events.

Selecting a Database

When you click the Find Database button of the program, DBAQUA.VBP on the companion disk, you bring up the common Open dialog box with two possible file types set: *.mdb for Access and *.dbf for FoxPro. When you select a file to open, the dialog box returns with cDlg.Filename set to a file name of one of these types. You can check for the extension type and set the database type accordingly. In addition, the names of the table and names fields differ and you can set them here. Then you can open the database as follows:

```
Private Sub Find_Click()
Dim i As Integer
If dbOpened Then db.Close    'close if one open already
'allow both types of files
cDlg.Filter = "Access database|*.mdb|FoxPro Database|*.dbf"
cDlg.ShowOpen
If Len(cDlg.filename) > 0 Then
 cfile.FullName = cDlg.filename
 i = InStr(cfile.FullName, ".dbf")
 If i > 0 Then
   dbFileName = cfile.PathName
   dbType = "FoxPro 2.5;"
   RecordName = "Athlete"        'table name
   FieldName = "Name"            'field name
   Query.Visible = True
 Else
   dbFileName = cfile.FullName
   dbType = ""             'if Access, leave blank
   RecordName = "Competitor"    'table name
   FieldName = "CompetitorName" 'field name
   Query.Visible = True
 End If
Set ws = DBEngine.Workspaces(0)
Set db = ws.OpenDatabase(dbFileName, False, False, dbType)
dbOpened = True
End If
End Sub
```

If you click the Get All Names button, it makes a list of the names of all the athletes in the competition:

```
Set Rec = db.OpenRecordset(RecordName, dbOpenDynaset)
```

Since these names are not sorted, create a second recordset with the names sorted, and then add the names from this sorted recordset into the list box:

```
'create new sorted record set
Rec.Sort = "[" + FieldName + "]"
Set SortRec = Rec.OpenRecordset
Do Until SortRec.EOF
  List1.AddItem SortRec(FieldName)
  SortRec.MoveNext
Loop
```

Note that you set the Sort property of the Rec recordset and use it to create the new sorted recordset. (Of course you could have sorted the original one by using a SQL query instead.)

Structures of the Databases

Even though you want to obtain the same information from both databases, their structure is quite different. In the FoxPro database, there is an Entries table that has the swimmers' names in one column and the event symbols in another column. The aquatics events have "AQ" as the first two characters of their symbolic name. Thus, you can select the athletes in aquatics events by selecting any row where the event ID starts with the letters "AQ." You easily can write the SQL query to select these rows and sort them alphabetically:

```
Set SelRec = db.OpenRecordset _
   "(SELECT DISTINCTROW ENTRIES.EVNTID," & _
   " ENTRIES.NAME From ENTRIES WHERE " & _
   "((ENTRIES.EVNTID Like 'AQ*')) ORDER BY ENTRIES.NAME;")
```

Structure of the Access database

By contrast, the Access database is much more complex. It consists of a large number of interrelated tables. To determine the names of the competitors and the names of the events they entered, you must access the Competitor, Athlete, CompetitorAssignment, AthleteEvents, and Event tables. These have related fields as follows:

Competitor
>   CompetitorName
>   CompetitorID

Athlete
>   AthleteID

CompetitorAssignment
>   AtheleteID
>   CompetitorID

AtheleteEvents
>   AtheleteID
>   EventID

Event
>   EventID
>   SportID

To determine who is entered in an aquatics event, you must find each competitor, trace the AtheleteID from the CompetitorID, find the AthleteEvents for that AthleteID and find the Event from that EventID. Any Event with a SportID of 1 is an aquatics event.

This is too complex a SQL statement for the untutored user. Instead, construct the SQL query using the Query By Example feature of Microsoft Access to connect the related tables visually, and then copy the SQL that was generated to the Clipboard and from there into the VB program. The generated statement is:

```
Set SelRec = db.OpenRecordset("SELECT DISTINCTROW " &_
  "Competitor.CompetitorName, Event.EventName " & _
  "FROM Event INNER JOIN ((Athlete INNER JOIN " & _
  "(Competitor INNER JOIN CompetitorAssignment " & _
  "ON Competitor.CompetitorID =" & _
  "CompetitorAssignment.CompetitorID) ON " & _
  "Athlete.AthleteID = " & _
  "CompetitorAssignment.AthleteID) INNER JOIN AthleteEvents
  ON " & _
  "Athlete.AthleteID = AthleteEvents.AthleteID)" & _
  "ON Event.EventID = AthleteEvents.EventID " & _
  "Where ((Event.SportID = 1)) ORDER BY
  Competitor.CompetitorName;")
```

To encapsulate the construction of these recordsets, build a class called AqEvents that receives the database name, selects the type of SQL statement, and sets the correct field names for filling the grid. The dbType Let property contains all these decisions:

```
Property Let dbType(dt$)
Dim i As Integer


i = InStr(dt$, "Fox")
If i > 0 Then
  NameField = "Name"
  EventField = "EvntID"
  Set SelRec = db.OpenRecordset("SELECT DISTINCTROW
   ENTRIES.EVNTID," &
   'etc. etc.
Else
  NameField = "CompetitorName"
  EventField = "EventName"
  Set SelRec = db.OpenRecordset("SELECT DISTINCTROW
     Competitor.CompetitorName, Event.EventName " & _
   'etc. etc.
End If


End Property
```

You also include a routine to fill the grid with competitor names and event names. It is entirely database-independent, using the NameField and EventField variables set earlier.

```
Public Sub FillGrid()
Dim srname$
Do Until SelRec.EOF
 frm.grid1.Row = frm.grid1.Rows - 1
 srname$ = SelRec(NameField)
 If Left$(srname$, 1) <> "0" Then    'leave out relays
   frm.grid1.Col = 0
   frm.grid1.Text = srname$
   frm.grid1.Col = 1
   frm.grid1.Text = SelRec(EventField)
   frm.grid1.AddItem ""
  End If
  SelRec.MoveNext
Loop
SelRec.Close


End Sub
```

The resulting display with the grid filled is shown in Figure 10-9.

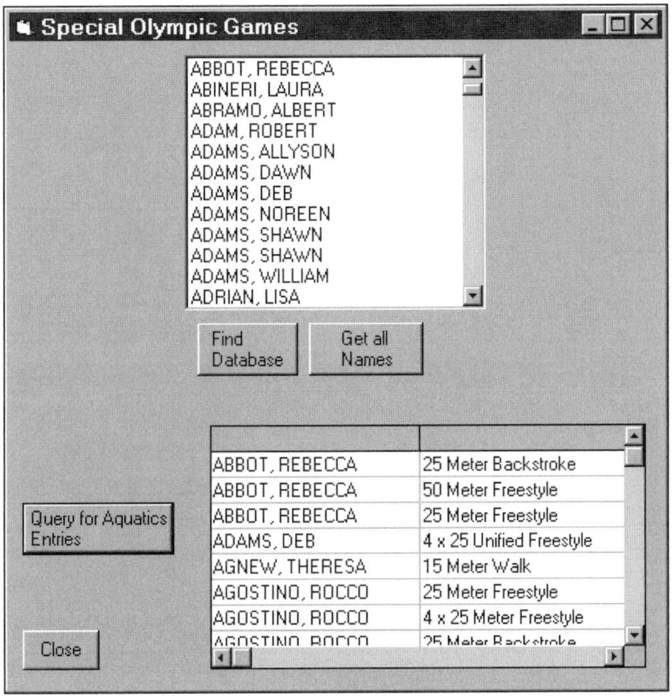

Figure 10-9.

***Display of the sorted
athletes, and of those
in aquatics events***

Figure 10-9.

Display of the sorted athletes, and of those in aquatics events

11 | Fonts and Printing

In MS-DOS–based BASIC programs, you usually issued a PRINT statement to list data on the screen, and an LPRINT statement to print data on the attached printer. You cannot do this directly in Visual Basic because of the flexibility of the Windows environment. In VB, you must indicate where you want to print the text, as well as in which font, size, and color.

In this chapter, we'll discuss how to handle Font objects and how to use them in printing data to printers as well as to the screen. You'll then see how to use object-oriented techniques to print labels.

You can use the Print method on forms, picture boxes, printer devices, and in the Debug window. Usually, printing is carried out within picture boxes, and on printers. Printing on forms is extremely rare, because forms are usually the background for a number of controls and such printing would be obscured by the controls.

Font Objects

A Font object is a set of specifications for displaying characters for Print methods and for the display of text in Captions and Text properties. The major properties of a font are shown in Table 11-1.

Table 11-1.

Font properties

FontName	The name of the font
Size	Size in points
Color	RGB color
Bold	**True or False**
Italic	*True or False*
Underline	<u>True or False</u>
StrikeThrough	~~True or False~~

All printers and the screen itself have a property array of fonts associated with them. You can list out the fonts that are available from the Fonts array:

```
For i = 0 To Screen.FontCount - 1
  fontlist.AddItem Screen.Fonts(i)
Next I
```

To set the display or printer to a particular font, set the name and size and then print:

```
'display font name in picture box
picture1.FontName = fontlist.Text
picture1.Font.Size = 12
picture1.Print fontlist.text
```

You also could print this text directly on the form:

```
'display on form
scrnfont.FontName = fontlist.Text
scrnfont.Font.Size = Font_size
scrnfont.Print picture1.FontName
```

However, you can only print 10 to 12 lines before the names disappear below the bottom of the form, and they cannot be scrolled back up. The program SCRNFONT.VBP on the companion disk illustrates these functions as shown in Figure 11-1.

Figure 11-1.

The SCRNFONT.VBP program

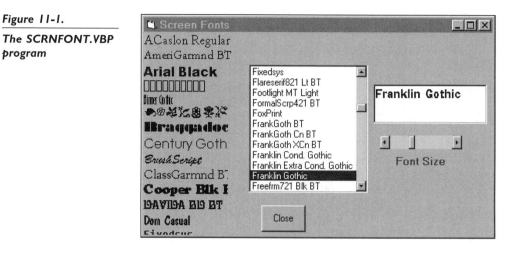

Printing Using the Printer Object

You can print on the current default printer by calling the Print method of the Printer object. Typical Basic syntax applies:

```
Printer.Print "Hello"  'print text and skip to new line
Printer.Print "Hello"; 'print text and stay on same line
Printer.Print "Hello", 'print text and skip to next tab
```

Since you can set the same font properties in the Printer object, you have a great deal of control over the appearance of your output, and you can make quite an elegant-looking presentation with only minimal programming.

The Printer object also has a Fonts property array, and it is important that you select a font that appears in this list rather than on the screen font list, to make the most accurate rendering on the page. If you select a font that the printer cannot print, Windows will attempt to select the closest matching font.

Visual Basic also contains a collection of all printers for which you have installed Windows drivers. You can enumerate this list and put it in a list box with the following code:

```
Dim pr As Printer
For Each pr In Printers
  Prnters.AddItem pr.DeviceName
Next pr
```

Then you can make that printer the currently selected printer with:

```
'select a new printer
Set Printer = Printers(Prnters.ListIndex)
'list out its fonts
For i = 0 To Printer.FontCount - 1
  Fnts.AddItem Printer.Fonts(i)
Next i
```

In the program PRNTFONT.VBP on the companion disk, I show how to enumerate both the existing printers and the existing fonts for a given printer, as well as change the font style to use Italic, Bold, and Underline properties. This is illustrated in Figure 11-2.

Figure 11-2.

Printer device names and the fonts available for a given printer

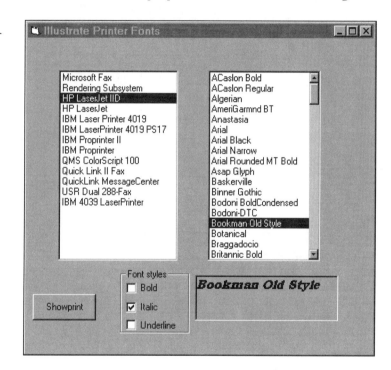

In the PRNTFONT.VBP program, the ShowPrint button brings up the Print Windows Common Dialog and allows you to select the current printer there as well.

Printer Object Properties

You can set and examine any of a large number of properties of the Printer object. Some of these are shown in Table 11-2.

ColorMode	True if printing in color (on a color printer)
Copies	An integer
Duplex	1=single-sided 2=double-sided, horizontal page turn 2=double-sided, vertical page turn
Orientation	1=portrait 2=landscape
PaperBin	1=upper 2=lower 3=middle 4=wait for hand feed 5=envelope feeder 8=pin feed see Help for nine more
PaperSize	1=Letter 5=Legal There are 42 styles supported. See Help.
TrackDefault	True if changing default in Control Panel changes printer

Printer Object Methods

To print on a printer, issue any number of Printer.Print statements. To begin a new page, use the Printer.NewPage method and when you finish, send the job to the printer using Printer.EndDoc. You also can stop a print job still spooling using Printer.KillDoc.

Graphics and Printing

Both the Screen (picture boxes) and Printer objects support the basic graphics methods: Pset, Line, and Circle. Using the CurrentX and CurrentY properties, you can either set or read the position on the page or screen; using the TextWidth and TextHeight methods, you can discover the size of text in the current font.

Thus, it is easy to print out text in a given font and then draw a box around it:

```
'print the text
Picture1.Print s$


'get current position
x = Picture1.CurrentX
y = Picture1.CurrentY


'calculate width and height of text
w = Picture1.TextWidth(s$)
h = Picture1.TextHeight(s$)


'Draw box around it
Picture1.Line (x, y)-(x - w, y + h), , B
```

This is illustrated in the TEXTBOX.VBP program on the companion disk and shown in Figure 11-3.

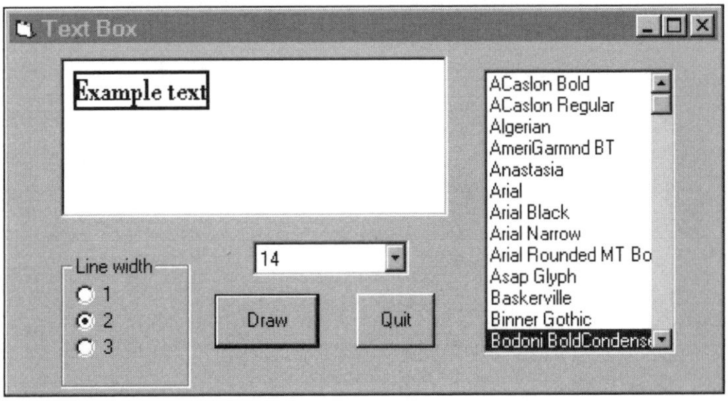

Figure 11-3.

Drawing a box around text in a picture box

Printing Labels

One of the most commonly requested features in Visual Basic programs is the ability to print labels from an application. These might be customer name and address labels, labels for file folders, or labels for handouts. Labels can be printed on pin-feed dot matrix printers or on laser printer labels. You need to be able to select the correct font, printer, layout, and page size for each type in a relatively "user-proof" manner. The label program presented below takes the members of the ever-popular customer file and prints their address labels on either a laser or a dot-matrix printer. For simplicity, assume 1-inch pin-feed labels and the rather standard two-column 4-inch-by-1-inch laser printer sheet labels.

Since programmers believe that an object should know best how to print itself, you will create an object that contains the customer list and knows how to print itself on both kinds of labels. So, while you may obtain the customer data list in the same manner as previously, you will pass a reference to that collection to the PrintLabel object to print. You will set the Printer object by selecting its name from a list box, but will pass whether to print two-column laser labels or one-column pin-feed labels to the PrintLabel object.

Determining sheet vs. pin-feed labels

In the list of installed printer drivers shown in Table 11-3, you can see that some are clearly laser printers and some clearly dot-matrix pin-feed printers.

Table 11-3.

Installed printer drivers

Printer	Port	Type
HP LaserJet II-d	LPT1	sheet
HP LaserJet	LPT1	sheet
IBM Proprinter II	LPT2	pin-feed
IBM Proprinter	LPT2	pin-feed
IBM 4019 PS17	LPT1	sheet
IBM 4039	LPT1	sheet
QMS ColorScript 100	LPT1	sheet
QuickLink Fax	COM3	*
User 288 Fax	COM3	*

Further, while you can eliminate the fax modem drivers by the port name they are connected to, we cannot *a priori* determine which are dot-matrix pin-feed printers and which are not.

You can determine which kind of printer you have by looking at the PaperBin property. One of its values (8) refers to pin-feed paper—only pin-feed printers can have this property. So, you can determine the type of printer by setting its PaperBin property and then looking for whether an error occurs:

```
On Local Error GoTo binerr
Printer.PaperBin = 8 'may cause error trap


If Printer.PaperBin = 8 Then
  pinfeed.Value = True 'pinfeed printer
Else
  laser.Value = True 'laser printer
  End If
Exit Sub
```

Continued on next page

```
binerr:        'error trap and return
 Resume Next
```

Printing laser printer labels

To print laser printer labels, alternate printing one in the left column
with one in the right column:

```
Private Sub print_laser_labels()
Dim Left As Boolean
'There are 1440 twips per inch
Dim x As Long, y As Long, i As Integer


Printer.CurrentY = 500        'skip top margin
Printer.CurrentX = leftside   'set left margin
Left = True                   'alternates
For i = 1 To clcust.Count
  Set Cust = clcust.Item(i)
  y = Printer.CurrentY        'save top of label
  print_customer              'print name & address
  If Left Then
    leftside = leftside + 4# * 1440
    Printer.CurrentY = y
    Printer.CurrentX = leftside
    Left = False
  Else
    Printer.CurrentY = y + 1440
    leftside = 100
    Left = True
  End If
Next i
End Sub
```

For simplicity I have omitted a check for when to eject the page.

Printing pin-feed labels

If you left the page size set to 8.5 by 11 inches, the printer driver
would cause a page eject every 10.5 inches, and you would skip a
couple of labels. This might not keep the labels lined up after the
page is ejected. Instead, set the page length to 1 inch and eject a
"page" after every label:

```
Private Sub print_pin_labels()
Dim i As Integer
Printer.Height = 1400    'one inch labels
For i = 1 To clcust.Count
  Set Cust = clcust.Item(i)
  print_customer              'print name and address
  Printer.NewPage
Next i
End Sub
```

The PrintLabels class

The rest of the class member functions are to set the printer type, pass in a reference to the Customers collection, and print the labels:

```
' class PrintLabels
Private clcust As Customers
Private laser_type As Boolean
Private leftside As Long
Private Cust As Customer
'_____
Property Set custlist(cl As Customers)
 Set clcust = cl
End Property
'_____
Property Let PrinterType(prtype As Boolean)
 laser_type = prtype 'true if laser
End Property
'_____
Public Sub PrintLabels()
leftside = 100
If laser_type Then
  print_laser_labels
Else
  print_pin_labels
End If
Printer.EndDoc
End Sub
```

Eliminate the fax-modem printers from the printer driver list by checking the printer port name, and displaying it only if it contains "LPT." The option buttons are not set by the user, but by setting the PaperBin property as illustrated earlier. The complete program is PRNTLABL.VBP on the companion disk, and is shown in Figure 11-4.

Figure 11-4.

The label printing program PRNTLABL.VBP

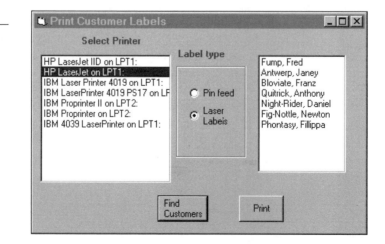

12 | Creating Matrix Objects

Matrixes, or two-dimensional arrays of numbers, are widely used in various fields of science and mathematics. Many matrixes are square (2 columns by 2 rows, 3 x 3, and so on) but they need not be. You can add, subtract, and multiply matrixes, as well as invert and diagonalize them. Thus, a matrix is an ideal example of the kind of abstraction encountered in object-oriented programming: the object itself is the best judge of how to carry out an operation on itself.

In addition, you have the additional challenge of designing an easy-to-use interface that will allow you to test these matrix classes and examine their results.

Matrix Terminology

Consider a general 3 x 3 matrix:

$$
\begin{bmatrix}
a_{11} & a_{12} & a_{13} \\
a_{21} & a_{22} & a_{23} \\
a_{31} & a_{32} & a_{33}
\end{bmatrix}
$$

This matrix is a square array of numbers having subscripts from 1 to 3 in both directions. In matrix algebra, you often represent a matrix by a single capital letter: A. If we have two such matrixes:

$$A = \begin{bmatrix} a_{11} & a_{12} \\ a_{21} & a_{22} \end{bmatrix} \qquad B = \begin{bmatrix} b_{11} & b_{12} \\ b_{21} & b_{22} \end{bmatrix}$$

we can write matrix addition as:

$C = A + B$

The C matrix then contains the cell-by-cell sum of the two arrays.

$$C = \begin{bmatrix} a_{11} + b_{11} & a_{12} + b_{12} \\ a_{21} + b_{21} & a_{22} + b_{22} \end{bmatrix}$$

Subtraction is carried out in an analogous fashion.

Matrix multiplication can occur only when the number of columns in the first matrix is equal to the number of rows in the second. Then the product A X can be obtained by multiplying each element in each row of the first matrix by each element in the corresponding column of the second matrix, and adding these products for a given row and column.

If A consists of m rows and B consists of n columns, then you construct the matrix C by multiplying each row of A into each column of B. The element C_{ij} is the product of the ith row of A and the jth column of B.

$$c_{ij} = \sum_{k=1}^{p} a_{ik} b_{kj}$$

Thus, the order of multiplication is important: the operation is not commutative.

Constructing a Matrix Class

Clearly a Matrix class with methods such as Add and Multiply seems like an ideal programming abstraction. Consider how this might be done. Suppose you wanted to add matrixes A and B together, and wanted the result in matrix C. Because there is no way to make the plus sign (+) operator carry out the Matrix Add method, there is no direct way to write:

```
matC = matA + matB
```

since there is no way to make the + operator carry out the Matrix Add method.

Instead, you need a way to create the *A* and *B* matrixes, and a way to tell one about the other:

```
Dim matA As New Matrix, matB as New Matrix
 matA.Fill                 'get data from somewhere
 matB.Fill                 'for each matrix
 Set matA.ymatrix = matB  'tell matA about 2nd matrix
 Set matC = matA.Add      'add them and put result in C
```

The critical point is that after you put that data in the two matrixes, you need a Property Set routine to set a reference to the second matrix within the first one, so it has two matrixes to operate on.

So your Matrix class must contain at least the following private variables:

```
Dim x() As Single       'the matrix data
Private y As Matrix      'reference to another matrix
Private xdim As Integer 'size of this matrix
Private ydim As Integer
Private z As Matrix      'an output matrix for results
```

Note that you are able to declare new instances of a matrix within the Matrix class itself. Then your Property Set routine has the form:

```
Property Set ymatrix(ymat As Matrix)
 Set y = ymat    'copy reference into this instance
End Property
```

The Item property

You need a method to obtain elements from a matrix so you can use them in another matrix's method. Utilize the Item property for this purpose:

```
Property Get Item(ByVal i As Integer, _
                 ByVal j As Integer) As Single
  Item = x(i, j)
End Property
'_____
Property Let Item(ByVal i As Integer, _
                 ByVal j As Integer, value As Single)
  x(i, j) = value
End Property
```

Then, using these methods, you can fetch the contents of matrix *B* from within matrix *A*.

Setting dimensions

You must set the dimensions of each matrix instance before performing any operations on it. Do this using the SetMatDim method:

```
Public Sub SetMatDim(ByVal i As Integer,_
                     ByVal j As Integer)
 xdim = i
 ydim = j
 ReDim x(xdim, ydim) As Single
End Sub
```

This stores the dimensions and then creates space for a matrix of those dimensions using the ReDim statement.

The Add method

Now you have enough information to create the Add method. Create a new output, matrix *Z*, of the same size as *A* and *B*, and store the addition results in it. Then return a reference to this new matrix as the function return:

```
Function Add() As Matrix
Dim i As Integer, j As Integer
  Set z = New Matrix          'create output matrix
  z.SetMatDim xdim, ydim      'define as same size
  For i = 1 To xdim           'perform addition
   For j = 1 To ydim
    z.Item(i, j) = x(i, j) + y.Item(i, j)
   Next j
  Next i
Set Add = z                   'return new matrix
End Function
```

The Subtract method works in a similar manner.

The Multiply method

You can do the same sort of thing for multiplication. You need two matrixes of the proper size, and must create an output matrix:

```
Function Multiply() As Matrix
Dim j As Integer, k As Integer
Dim col1 As Integer, col2 As Integer, col3 As Integer
Dim row1 As Integer, row2 As Integer, row3 As Integer
Dim i As Integer
Dim mSum As Single
row1 = xdim
col1 = ydim
Call y.GetMatDim(row2, col2)
'First matrix must have number of columns
'equal to number of rows in second matrix
```

Continued on next page

```
If col1 = row2 Then
 'The number of rows in the product matrix
 'must be equal to the number of rows in the first
 'and the number of columns = number of columns in 2nd
 Set z = New Matrix
 row3 = row1
 col3 = col2
 Call z.SetMatDim(row3, col3)
 For i = 1 To row1
   For j = 1 To col2
     mSum = 0
     For k = 1 To col1
        mSum = mSum + x(i, k) * y.Item(k, j)
     Next k
   z.Item(i, j) = mSum
  Next j
 Next i
 Set Multiply = z
End If
End Function
```

Inverting Matrixes

While dividing matrixes is not a meaningful operation, matrix inversion is very useful. If you define the unit matrix I as a matrix having 1s in the diagonal and 0s everywhere else:

$$I = \begin{bmatrix} 1 & 0 & 0 & 0 \\ 0 & 1 & 0 & 0 \\ 0 & 0 & 1 & 0 \\ 0 & 0 & 0 & 1 \end{bmatrix}$$

then you can define the inverse of a matrix A^{-1} as that matrix which, when multiplied by the original matrix A, produces the unity matrix I.

$A \times A^{-1} = I$

You can use matrix inversion as a convenient way to solve simultaneous equations. Suppose you have a series of simultaneous equations such as:

$$a_1 x_1 + b_1 x_2 + c_1 x_3 = k_1$$
$$a_2 x_1 + b_2 x_2 + c_2 x_3 = k_2$$
$$a_3 x_1 + b_3 x_2 + c_3 x_3 = k_3$$

You can write this in matrix form as:

$$\begin{bmatrix} a_1 & b_1 & c_1 \\ a_2 & b_2 & c_2 \\ a_3 & b_3 & c_3 \end{bmatrix} \begin{bmatrix} x_1 \\ x_2 \\ x_3 \end{bmatrix} = \begin{bmatrix} k_1 \\ k_2 \\ k_3 \end{bmatrix}$$

or just as:

$$MX = K$$

where M is the matrix of coefficients, X the column matrix of variables and K the column matrix of constants. Rearranging this simple equation you have:

$$M^{-1}K = X$$

So, if you can determine the inverse of the M matrix, you can solve for the x's.

Solving a set of simultaneous equations

Consider the three equations:

$$5x_1 + 3x_2 - 4x_3 = -10$$
$$3x_1 + 7x_2 + x_3 = 23$$
$$3x_1 - 3x_2 + 2x_3 = 20$$

You can rewrite these as a matrix algebra statement as:

$$\begin{bmatrix} 5 & 3 & -4 \\ 3 & 7 & 1 \\ 3 & -3 & 2 \end{bmatrix} \begin{bmatrix} x_1 \\ x_2 \\ x_3 \end{bmatrix} = \begin{bmatrix} -10 \\ 23 \\ 20 \end{bmatrix}$$

Thus, if you can invert this matrix, and multiply it by the constant column matrix, you can solve for the values of x.

The matrix Invert method follows one given by K.J. Johnson in Numerical *Methods in Chemistry* and by J.W. Cooper in *Visual Basic for DOS: Building Scientific and Technical Applications,* and is given on the companion disk in the program MATRIX.VBP. It returns the inverted matrix in place rather than in a new matrix.

If we put the matrix data into this routine, invert it, and multiply by the column vector -10, 23, 20, we find that:

$$x_1 = 3$$
$$x_2 = 1$$
$$x_3 = 7$$

Developing a User Interface

By now, you certainly realize that developing an easy-to-use interface is as much or more work than the writing of the computational and file-handling code commonly thought of as the guts of a program. The interface shown in Figure 12-1 consists of three Grid controls, two entry fields above the two input grids, four spin buttons for increasing or decreasing the number of rows and columns in a grid, and four command buttons labeled: + , -, X and ÷. The plus, minus, and multiply are obvious. You use the division sign to indicate matrix inversion.

Figure 12-1.

The matrix inversion user interface

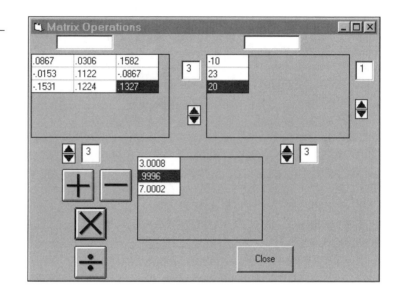

The screen in Figure 12-1 shows the results of inverting the matrix, as discussed in "Solving a set of simultaneous equations," followed by multiplying it by the column matrix to calculate the final values for x_1, x_2, and x_3.

Control arrays

The three grids, as well as the two entry fields and the Spin buttons, are designed as control arrays so that you needn't write the same code more than once for the two grids.

Using the Spin buttons

A Spin button contains up and down scroll arrows to indicate increasing and decreasing some quantity. It has two events—SpinUp and SpinDown—that occur when you click the upper and lower scroll arrows. You write an event procedure to increment and decrement the number of rows or columns in each grid:

```
Private Sub SpinRow_SpinUp(Index As Integer)
Dim r As Integer
'Increment the number of grid rows
 r = Grid1(Index).Rows
 Grid1(Index).Rows = r + 1
 txrows(Index).Text = Str$(r + 1)
End Sub
'_____
Private Sub SpinRow_SpinDown(Index As Integer)
Dim r As Integer
'Decrement the number of grid rows
r = Grid1(Index).Rows
If r > 1 Then
 Grid1(Index).Rows = r - 1
End If
txrows(Index).Text = Str$(r - 1)
End Sub
```

Entering data in the grid

The grid itself does not allow you to type in data values, so you provide a text entry field associated with each grid. To use it, start in the upper left corner and type values followed by pressing ENTER. Each press of ENTER places that value into a grid cell and you advance to the next cell. Do this by trapping the Enter (ASCII 13) character in the KeyDown event.

```
Private Sub txGrid_KeyDown(Index As Integer, _
                KeyCode As Integer, Shift As Integer)
Dim c As Integer, r As Integer
If KeyCode = 13 Then        ' if Enter save value
  Grid1(Index).Text = txGrid(Index).Text
  txGrid(Index).Text = "" 'clear box after copy
  KeyCode = 0              'return no character
  c = Grid1(Index).Col
  'Increment to next column
  If c < Grid1(Index).Cols - 1 Then
    Grid1(Index).Col = c + 1
  Else
    'and to next row if at end of column
    r = Grid1(Index).Row
    If r < Grid1(Index).Rows - 1 Then
      Grid1(Index).Col = 0
      Grid1(Index).Row = r + 1
    End If
  End If
  'Highlight new cell
  Grid1(Index).SelStartRow = Grid1(Index).Row
```

Continued on next page

```
    Grid1(Index).SelEndRow = Grid1(Index).Row
    Grid1(Index).SelStartCol = Grid1(Index).Col
    Grid1(Index).SelEndCol = Grid1(Index).Col
End If
End Sub
```

Clicking the grid

Whenever you click a number in one of the entry grids, it is copied to the text box above so you can edit it.

Reading data into a matrix from a grid

Here are methods for copying data into a matrix from a grid, and vice-versa. These are public methods of the Matrix class and require that you pass in a Grid control. The FillFromGrid subroutine follows:

```
Public Sub FillFromGrid(Gr As Grid)
Dim i As Integer, j As Integer
'Fills matrix from input grid
 Call SetMatDim(Gr.Rows, Gr.Cols)
 For i = 0 To Gr.Rows - 1
   For j = 0 To Gr.Cols - 1
     Gr.Row = i
     Gr.Col = j
     x(i + 1, j + 1) = Val(Gr.Text)
   Next j
Next i
End Sub
```

13 | Debugging Visual Basic Programs

As soon as you begin programming, you will encounter problems with your programs: mistakes, bugs, crashes, and unexpected results.

Run-Time Errors

The first kind of errors you may encounter are errors the compiler finds in trying to compile your code. Many of these are fairly obvious from the error message the compiler generates. A few, however, are a bit confusing. Consider the following program fragment from the program DEBUG1.VBP (on the companion disk) with a number of errors in it:

```
Dim cfile As clsFile
Dim cust As Customer
Dim Customers As Collection
'_____
Private Sub Openit_Click()
cDlg.Filter = "Customers|*.add"
cDlg.ShowOpen
cfile.FullName = cDlg.filename
cfile.OpenInput
  If cfile.ErrorVal = 0 Then
    While Not cfile.EndFile
      Set cust = New Customer    'new customer object
      ReadCust cust              'read in data
      Customers.Add (cust)       'add to collection
      List1.AddItem cust.LastFirst
```

Continued on next page

```
      Wend
      cfile.CloseFile
    End If
End Sub
```

The program stops during execution with the error "Object variable or With block not set" on the highlighted line:

```
cfile.FullName = cDlg.filename
```

In this case, the error means that cfile is an Object variable and it is indeed not set. I should have declared a New object to actually create one. Let's correct that and go on:

```
Dim cust As Customer
Dim Customers As Collection
Dim cfile As New clsFile
'_____

Private Sub Openit_Click()
cDlg.Filter = "Customers|*.add"
cDlg.ShowOpen
cfile.FullName = cDlg.filename
cfile.OpenInput
  If cfile.ErrorVal = 0 Then
'  etc.
```

Now, when you execute the program, the File/Open dialog box comes up, but when you select the people.add file and click Open, you get the error message "Object does not support this property or method," with the Customers.Add line (shown in bold) when you click Debug:

```
While Not cfile.EndFile
   Set cust = New Customer    'make a new customer object
   ReadCust cust              'read in data
   Customers.Add (cust)       'add to collection
   List1.AddItem cust.LastFirst
Wend
```

This particular error can be maddeningly difficult to see, because it is so obvious: the problem is the parentheses around the cust class instance. The correct way to call a subroutine is either:

```
Call Customers.Add (cust)
```

or

```
Customers.Add cust
```

If you accidentally write:

```
Customers.Add (cust)
```

you are telling Visual Basic to evaluate cust as an *expression*. Then it tries to take that evaluation and add it to the collection. This is not allowed: Collections can contain either objects or variables of type Variant and the evaluation is neither of these. To correct the problem, remove the parentheses.

The Visual Basic Debug Window

One way to monitor what is happening while a program is running is to print out variables in the Debug window. The statement Debug.Print will print a variable or list of variables in the Debug window. This window is scrollable, so you can stop at any time, scroll back up, and look at previously printed data.

A Fibonacci series

Suppose you want to write a program to display the first dozen or so components of the Fibonacci series: 1, 1, 2, 3, 5, 8, and so on, where each term is the sum of the previous two. You write what you believe is a correct program to add these terms together:

```
Private Sub Startit_Click()
Dim i As Integer, j As Integer, num As Integer
Dim last As Integer
last = 0              'previous term
num = 1               'current term
List1.AddItem Str$(num) 'list initial value
last = num
num = num + last        'add to get 2nd term


While num < 100         'loop until >100
  List1.AddItem Str$(num)
  last = num            'make current term last
  num = num + last      'add to get next term
Wend


End Sub
```

This program is called FIBO.VBP on the companion disk. Unfortunately, the result this program displays in the list box is:

```
1
2
4
8
16
32
64
```

which is clearly incorrect. So you resort to debugging. First, set a breakpoint inside the While loop on:

```
num = num + last      'add to get next term
```

by moving the cursor to it and pressing F9 to set a breakpoint. Then start the program by pressing F5 and examine the state of the variables at the breakpoint. Click the program's Start button, and a breakpoint occurs immediately at the line indicated earlier. You can go to the Debug window and examine the variables by typing the command:

```
print num, last
```

and discovering that the variables are both 2, as shown in Figure 13-1.

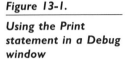

Figure 13-1.

Using the Print statement in a Debug window

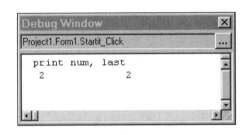

Or you can set two Watchpoints by selecting Add Watch from the Tools menu, and entering *num* and *last* as variables to watch, as shown in Figure 13-2.

Figure 13-2.

Watching the num and last variables

Watchpoints are useful if you must step through several iterations to see what's going on. For example, if you press F5 to continue, the program will go through the While loop once and stop again, showing the Watchpoints as 4 and 4. In any case, the algorithm is clearly wrong and you have to redesign it. The problem is that you copy the value of *num* to *last* before you add, and thus you always are doubling the value of *num*. After a little head scratching, you realize that you must keep the two previous terms in two separate variables, and that the correct solution is actually shorter:

```
Private Sub Startit_Click()
Dim i As Integer, j As Integer, num As Integer
Dim last As Integer, seclast As Integer
last = 0            'previous term
seclast = 0
num = 1                'current term


While num < 100           'loop until >100
  List1.AddItem Str$(num)
  seclast = last
  last = num
  num = last + seclast     'add to get next term
Wend


End Sub
```

This corrected program is called FIBO1.VBP on the companion disk.

Debugging OLE Servers

While it is often possible to write test programs that you can compile along with the OLE server code and test as part of a single process, it occasionally happens that a bug appears after a substantial amount of client code has been written, and you need to find out what's going on inside the OLE server to explain your problem.

This is easy to do in VB 4, because you can run two copies of VB at once—one running the server and another running the client—and place breakpoints in both. They can even be different versions of VB (16- and 32-bit).

Be careful, though—you must set your breakpoints and start your OLE server code first. Minimize the server instance of Visual Basic and start another one for the client.

Then select the correct version of the library from the Tools/References window in the client VB session. A line at the bottom of the window shows the location of the server code; make sure it shows server.*vbp* rather than server.*exe* or .*dll*. Then set any desired breakpoints in the client code and start it as well.

14 | Multimedia Object Programming

There are two simple ways to play and record sound clips, and to play back video clips, in Visual Basic. The simplest method uses the Multimedia MCI control; the next simplest is to make calls directly using Media Control Interface (MCI) strings. MCI strings are a set of simple commands you can send to Windows to open, play, and record media files. The commands are of the form "open," "play," "stop," and "close." The Multimedia MCI control sends predetermined MCI strings to the underlying Windows multimedia system.

The brief tour in this chapter also will give you a chance to show how to call functions in existing Windows DLLs, and how to decide whether to call the 16-bit or 32-bit DLL.

The Multimedia MCI Control

Start by placing the Multimedia MCI control on a form and see how you can use it. This control usually is not in the default set, but you can add it to your toolbox by choosing Custom Controls from the Tools menu and selecting the line labeled "Microsoft Multimedia Control." This will add an icon to the toolbox window that contains a note and some other hard-to-see drawings. Click this new toolbox button and place one on a form as shown in Figure 14-1.

Figure 14-1.

An MCI control placed on a form

The controls are VCR-like and represent the following operations:

- Previous
- Next
- Play
- Pause
- Back
- Step
- Stop
- Record
- Eject

Each of these has an Enabled and a Visible property. The control also has an AutoEnable property, which will enable those functions that are appropriate for a given media file type. In general, the Previous, Next, Step, and Eject buttons are irrelevant. In this example, I have named this control mm. Since you will need to select a file to play, place a Common Dialog control on the form as well.

Types of multimedia files

The MCI control supports the file types shown in Table 14-1, if appropriate drivers have been installed.

Table 14-1.

File types supported by the MCI control

String	Description
AVIVideo	(Video for Windows)
CDAudio	Music on your CDRom drive
DAT	Digital audio tape
DigitalVideo	Digital video files
MMMovie	Multimedia movie files
Other	Other file types
Overlay	Overlay files
Scanner	Scanner input
Sequencer	MIDI sequencer
VCR	Input from a VCR
Videodisc	Input from a videodisc player
WaveAudio	Wave files

To select which type you want to play, set the DeviceType property to one of the strings in Table 14-1. In the example program on the companion disk, you decide on the basis of the file extension:

```
'decide which type based on filename extension
Select Case LCase$(cFile.Extension)
Case "wav"
  mm.DeviceType = "WaveAudio"
Case "mid"
  mm.DeviceType = "Sequencer"
Case "avi"
  mm.DeviceType = "AVIVideo"
End Select
```

Now, to read in and play a sound file, you need only to select that file and set the filename property of the multimedia control. You also must set a few other properties to standard values:

```
'set the MCI Control
mm.filename = cdlg.filename
mm.Wait = True    'wait to finish current MCI command
mm.Shareable = False 'programs cannot share device
mm.Command = "Open"
mm.Notify = True      'generates a "Done" event
```

Once you have set a file name into the control, and sent the "Open" command as shown previously, the allowed buttons of the control will become enabled and you can play back a wave file, a MIDI file, or an AVI (movie) file. A short example of each is provided in the DATA folder, and you should be able to play all three of them on most Windows-based computers.

The MCI String Interface

While in many programs it is adequate to use the Multimedia MCI control, there are times when you'd just like to send the multimedia commands yourself, so that a program can play sound files without needing a user to click a button on a player.

To make use of the MCI commands, you must tell Visual Basic which DLL they are located in and what the calling arguments are. A Windows API Text Viewer program is provided with both versions of Visual Basic, and you can easily select and insert the correct commands for either version. Since you want the multimedia class to work in either environment, you must include an conditional compilation #if statement that tests for whether Win16 or Win32 is true and uses the correct set of declare statements:

```
#If Win16 Then
  Declare Function mciGetErrorString Lib "mmsystem" (ByVal
    wError As _
                    Long, ByVal str$, ByVal uLength As Integer) As
    Integer


  Declare Function mciSendString Lib "mmsystem" (ByVal
    lpstrCommand As _
      String, ByVal lpstrReturnString As String, ByVal
    uReturnLength _
      As Integer, ByVal hwndCallback As Integer) As Long
#Else
  Declare Function mciSendString Lib "winmm.dll" Alias _
    "mciSendStringA" (ByVal lpstrCommand As String, ByVal str$, _
    ByVal uReturnLength As Long, ByVal hwndCallback As Long)
    As Long


  Declare Function mciGetErrorString Lib "winmm.dll" Alias _
    "mciGetErrorStringA" (ByVal dwError As Long, ByVal lpstrBuffer_
    As String, ByVal uLength As Long) As Long
#End If
```

While there are a large number of MCI commands in these DLLs, we only need two of them, mmsystem.dll and winmm.dll. To send a command to the interface, just reserve space for the return information and send the command:

```
mciReturn = String$(256, " ")
mcireturnlength = 256
mciErrString = String$(256, " ")
mcierrlength = 256
mciError = mciSendString(mcicommand, mciReturn, mcireturnlength,
   hWnd)
If mciError < 0 Then
  ans = mciGetErrorString(mciError, mciErrString,mcierrlength)
  MsgBox Left$(mciErrString, mcierrlength - 1)
End If
```

Fortunately you can encapsulate the entire function in a class. The MultiMed class you are creating has the two simple methods shown in Table 14-2.

Table 14-2.

MultiMed class methods

Play(file$)	Plays the file specified
SetPlay(OnOff)	Turns off sound

To play files of any type, execute the code:

```
Dim Media As New MultiMed


Private Sub Playit_Click()
  Media.Play cFile.FullName
End Sub
```

Any file for which a driver has been installed will be played or displayed.

The following Play method calls the SendString function shown previously:

```
Public Sub Play(ByVal file$)
If sound_flag Then
  file$ = sound_dir + file$
  Call Play_sound(file$)
 End If
End Sub
'_____

Private Sub Play_sound(wavefile$)
 Call mciSend("open " + wavefile$ + " alias wfile")
 Call mciSend("play wfile wait")
 Call mciSend("close wfile")
End Sub
```

While the code indicates that only sounds can be played, it actually works for all media types.

Include the SetPlay method so all sounds you might have the program play can be turned off by setting a flag. Thus, the code to play the sounds remains intact, but the class itself skips playing if this Boolean is set to False. This is ideal for development environments, where you might get sick of hearing the sounds.

The program PLAYSND.VBP on the companion disk will play data both using the MCI Control and the MCI string interface directly. If your computer has no sound card, a speaker driver is widely available as freeware and gives you some idea how the sounds would play on a real sound card. For Windows 95, you can obtain this driver from:

- **CompuServe**
  GO MSL
  Search for Speak.exe
  Display results and download

- **Microsoft Download Service (MSDL)**

  Dial (206) 936-6735 to connect to MSDL

  Download Speak.exe

- **Internet (anonymous FTP)**

  ftp ftp.microsoft.com

  Change to the Softlib/Mslfiles directory

  Get Speak.exe

Conclusion

This modern version of Visual Basic finally brings the advantages of object-oriented programming to a much wider user community. You should by now be able to see some of the distinct advantages this style of programming has over conventional procedural programming, and can now begin incorporating this style into your own programs.

Just as you can write ordinary C code in the middle of a C++ program, you can write ordinary procedural VB code in the middle of a VB4 OO program. However, while you can mix styles, the advantages of OO design can quickly become lost. I encourage you to think through new projects and project revisions in terms of objects before you begin coding—the reliability and flexibility of the resulting programs will be worth the effort.

Appendix A

The Example Disk

Installing the Data on the Program Disk

The files on the companion disk are zipped into a single self-extracting PKZIP file. To unpack these programs, create a program example directory at the MS-DOS prompt:

```
md vbooprog
cd vbooprog
```

Then unzip the files into that directory by running:

```
a:vbooprog.exe
```

Disk Organization

Each chapter in the text is represented by a separate folder on the disk. All the data files the various programs require are stored in the DATA folder. The databases used in Chapter 10 are found in the ACCESS and FOXBASE folders within the DATA folder. Table A-1 provides a guide to the example programs used in this book.

Table A-1.

Guide to example programs

Chapter	Program	32-bit	Description
2	TEMPCALC		Converts between Fahrenheit and Celsius
	TEMPENTR		Converts and plots temperatures
	CONTROLS		Example of all common controls
3	RECTNGL1		Draws and moves a rectangle
	RECTNGL2		Draws and moves a rectangle using a structure to hold the data
	RECTNGL3		Draws and moves a rectangle using a Rectangle class
4	TEMPENTR		Accepts and plots temperatures using Public properties of plot form
	TEMPCOL		Accepts and plots temperatures, storing them in a collection
	CUSTOMER		Displays customer list and details
	CUSTTAG		Displays customer list and details using collection key
	TIMING		Calculates timing of creating and scanning arrays and collections, using several methods
5	SQUARES		Moves a square, derived from a Rectangle class
	SWIMMEET		Reads in a meet file and swimmer data files and displays the swimmers in any given event
	SWIMEET1		A slightly faster version of SWIMMEET, where the data is not converted to its internal representation until needed
6	DRAGDROP	32-bit	Allows viewing of files and customer data using a drag-and-drop interface
7	DRAWSHP	32-bit	Uses Sheridan Class Assistant to derive a Square class from a Rectangle class
	BLDLIST	32-bit	Uses Sheridan Class Assistant to build a list box with some bold entries

Continued on next page

8	LISTFORM	32-bit	Illustrates how to use a ListView control and drag-and-drop
	TREEFORM	32-bit	Shows use of TreeView control to display a table of contents tree
9	CUSTCLAS		An OLE server
	CUSTTEST		Test program for testing OLE server with client within same code
	OUTPTEST		Tests out-of-process OLE server
	INPTEST		Tests in-process OLE server
10	DBGRID		Displays competitor records from an Access database
	DBGRID1		Displays selected records from an Access database using SQL
	ENUMRATE		Displays selected records from Access database
	DBAQUA		Displays data from either Access or FoxPro databases
11	SCRNFONT		Displays fonts for screen in various sizes
	PRNTFONT		Displays fonts for selected printer
	TEXTBOX		Draws box around text using any selected font or line width
	PRNTLABL		Prints labels on pin-feed or laser printer from customer data file
12	MATRIX		Visual interface for matrix class that includes addition, subtraction, multiplication, and inversion
13	DEBUG1		Buggy program example
	FIBO		Buggy Fibonacci series program
	FIBO1		Corrected Fibonacci series program
14	PLAYSND		Multimedia player program for playing wave, MIDI, and AVI files

Index

About the Author

James W. Cooper is the author of nine previous books in the fields of computers and science. He is a research staff member at IBM's Thomas J. Watson Research Center. He received his Ph.D. in chemistry from Ohio State University. He is also the author of the leading Windows software package for competitive swimming, which was used at the Special Olympics World Games and which he provides as shareware.